CROCHET EDGINGS & TRIMS

CROCHET EDGINGS & TRIMS

150 designs for beautiful decorative edgings,
from lacy borders to bobbles, braids
and fringes

Susan Smith

SEARCH
PRESS

A QUARTO BOOK

Published in 2007 by Search Press Ltd.
Wellwood
North Farm Road
Tunbridge Wells
Kent TN2 3DR
United Kingdom

ISBN-10: 1-84448-197-2
ISBN-13: 978-1-84448-197-2

Conceived, designed and produced by
Quarto Publishing plc
The Old Brewery
6 Blundell Street
London N7 9BH

QUAR: CTR

Project Editor: Lindsay Kaubi
Art Editor: Jacqueline Palmer
Designer: Susi Martin
Assistant Art Director: Penny Cobb
Illustrator: Coral Mula
Pattern Checker: Helen Jordan
Photographers: Phil Wilkins and Paul Forrester
Proofreader: Christine Vaughan
Indexer: Diana LeCore

Art Director: Moira Clinch
Publisher: Paul Carslake

Manufactured by Modern Age Repro House Ltd., Hong Kong
Printed by SNP Leefung printers Ltd., China

10 9 8 7 6 5 4 3 2 1

CONTENTS

AUTHOR'S FOREWORD · 6
ABOUT THIS BOOK · 6

DIRECTORY OF TRIMS · 8

- EDGINGS · 10
- FRINGES · 18
- BRAIDS · 26
- MOTIFS · 31
- ACCESSORIES · 40

TECHNICAL DATA · 46

- EDGINGS · 48
- FRINGES · 58
- BRAIDS · 67
- MOTIFS · 74
- ACCESSORIES · 87

PROJECTS · 98

- BOBBLE BOLERO · 100
- POSY-EDGED CARDIGAN · 102
- FRILLED CUSHION · 104
- DOUBLE-TRIMMED SKIRT · 106
- EMBELLISHED BERET · 108

REFRESHER COURSE · 110

- MATERIALS AND EQUIPMENT · 112
- BASIC SKILLS · 114
- STITCHES · 115
- JOINING YARNS · 117
- TEXTURED STITCHES · 118
- MAKING A FRINGE · 119
- WORKING IN ROUNDS · 120
- THREE-DIMENSIONAL MOTIFS · 120
- MAKING CROCHET BUTTONS · 121
- APPLYING BEADS · 122
- APPLYING SEQUINS · 123
- WEB RESOURCES · 123
- MEASURING TENSION · 124
- BLOCKING · 124
- ENGLISH/AMERICAN TERMINOLOGY · 125
- CROCHET AFTERCARE · 125
- STANDARD CROCHET ABBREVIATIONS · 125

INDEX · 126
CREDITS · 128

AUTHOR'S FOREWORD

I am extremely passionate about crafts and have been crocheting for as long as I can remember. For me, creating something is as much about enjoying the journey as it is about the final product. I believe that any item that is hand crafted is a unique creation to be treasured.

This book is not only for those with lots of crochet experience but also for beginners. The vast, diverse and beautiful selection of crochet trims featured in this book range from the very easy to make to the complex and challenging; however, the nature of the book allows anyone — no matter how experienced or inexperienced a crocheter — to embellish an item with a decorative trim. Hopefully this book will also encourage readers to start creating and designing their own crochet work.

Susan Smith

ABOUT THIS BOOK

The book begins with a stunning visual directory of 150 crochet trims: once you've chosen the trim you'd like to make, use the handy trim reference number to locate its pattern in the Technical Data chapter. In the Projects chapter you will discover five inspirational project ideas for using and applying the trims. At the end of the book the Refresher Course contains all the basic information and crochet skills needed to work all the trims in the book: all techniques are clearly explained with step-by-step instructions and illustrations.

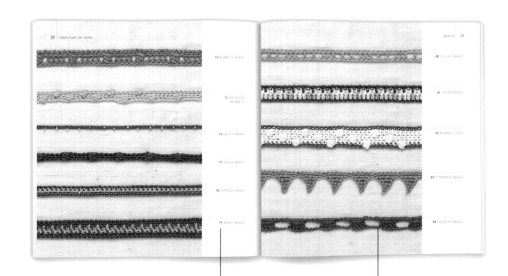

SECTION 1: DIRECTORY OF TRIMS

The Directory of Trims is a visual showcase of 150 crochet trims and is organized into five sub-sections: edgings, fringes, braids, motifs and accessories. Each trim is displayed actual size — just flick through and pick your trim.

Each trim is labelled with a trim number that corresponds to its pattern in the Technical Data chapter.

Trims are shown actual size.

SECTION 2: TECHNICAL DATA

Here, you'll find the patterns for every single trim along with information on the yarns, beads and sequins used to make each trim. There is also a detailed picture of each trim, going in closer than the directory so that you can see the stitches in detail. The Technical Data section is also organized into the five trim sections and each trim is labelled with its trim number as well as a page reference telling you where it is in the directory.

SECTION 3: PROJECTS

There are five attractive and inspirational projects ranging from a beret embellished with a floral motif to a silky cushion with a funky textured fringe. All of the projects are designed to encourage you to try using the trims in the book and to experiment with varying the colours, textures, beads and sequins used.

Each pattern appears in full.

Every trim pattern is rated according to skill level: beginner/easy, intermediate or challenging/complex.

Use the trim number to refer back to the actual size trim photograph in the directory.

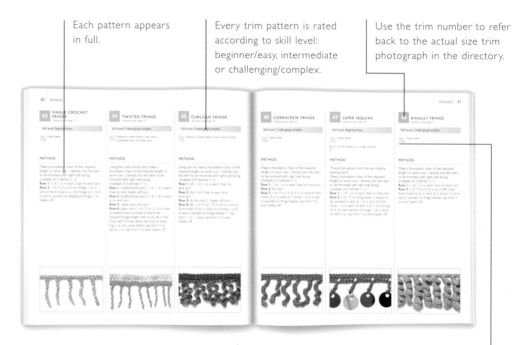

Instructions list the trims used, the materials needed and how to make and attach the trim.

Each project is illustrated with an inspirational picture of the finished item.

UNDERSTANDING THE SYMBOLS

Each trim pattern is accompanied by one or two symbols indicating the materials needed and, in some cases, the application for the trim.

Yarn used

Bead, sequin or finding used

Application/use for trim.

SECTION 4: REFRESHER COURSE

The Refresher Course guides you step-by-step through all the crochet basics in easy to follow sequences: from choosing a hook and yarn and basic stitches to working textured stitches and three-dimensional motifs.

DIRECTORY OF TRIMS

Most of us have something to which we'd like to add a personal touch: clothing bought impulsively; an old favourite that needs a new lease of life, or maybe a plain piece of knitting or crochet that would be beautifully complemented with a trim. Explore this stunning visual directory of 150 crocheted edgings, fringes, braids, motifs and accessories and you're sure to find the trim to suit you. Each beautifully photographed trim is displayed actual size and labelled with a trim number that corresponds to its pattern in the Technical Data chapter (pages 46–97), so that once you've chosen your trim you can flip directly to the pattern.

EDGINGS

Crochet edgings attached to a hem or seam can be used to fantastic effect to complement a fabric garment or soft furnishing. Edgings can be used on their own but can also be used in groups where they can interact visually to create interesting and textural patterns (see pages 106–107).

TO MAKE:

For edging patterns, see pages 48–57

I SHELL EDGE

2 SCALLOP EDGE

3 GLITZY EDGE

4 LARGE PICOT EDGE

5 BLOCK EDGE

6 SHELLS AND BEADS

7 REGULAR WAVES

8 FUZZY EDGE

9 ARCADE EDGE

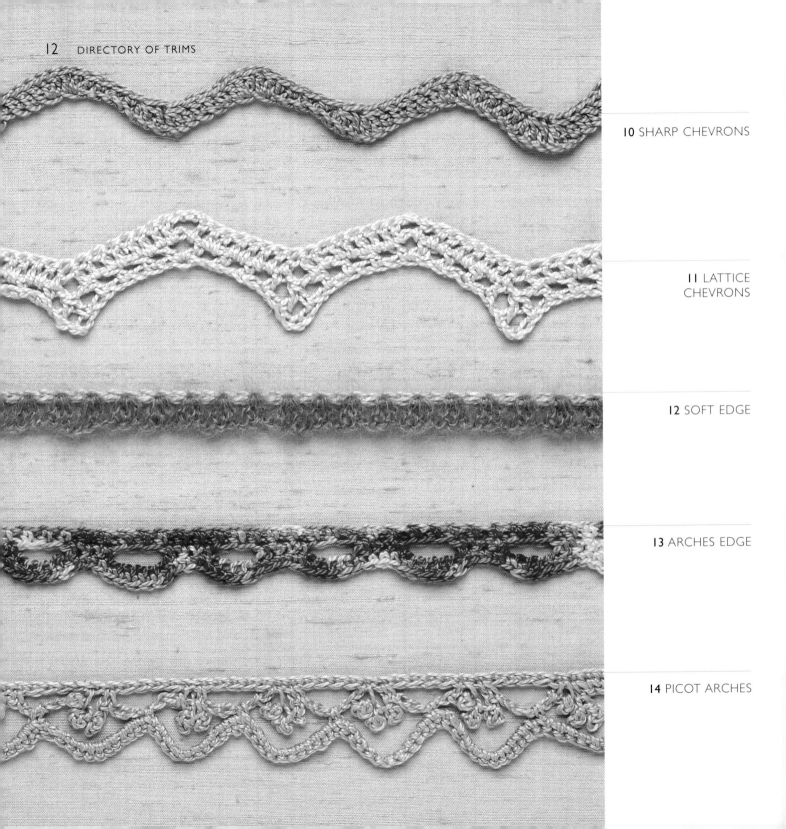

10 SHARP CHEVRONS

11 LATTICE
CHEVRONS

12 SOFT EDGE

13 ARCHES EDGE

14 PICOT ARCHES

15 RHYTHMIC EDGE

16 BEADED WAVES

17 SCALLOPED
ARCHES

18 ARCH AND
PICOT EDGE

19 SHALLOW
SCALLOPS

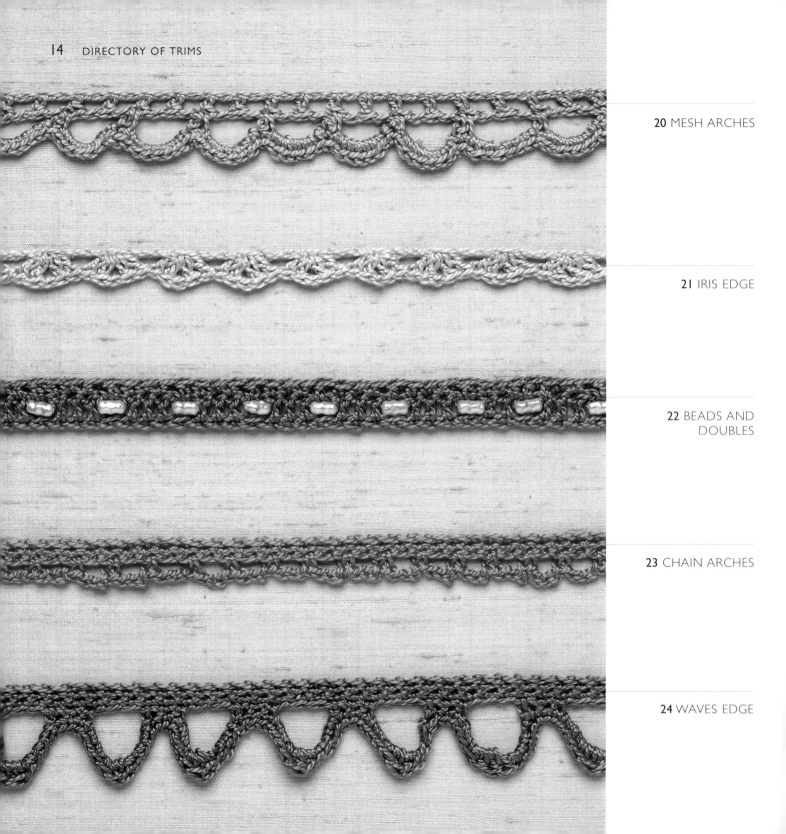

20 MESH ARCHES

21 IRIS EDGE

22 BEADS AND
DOUBLES

23 CHAIN ARCHES

24 WAVES EDGE

25 LAYERED CHAINS

26 SIMPLY BEADS

27 FLORAL EDGE

28 POSY EDGE

29 IRIS STITCH EDGE

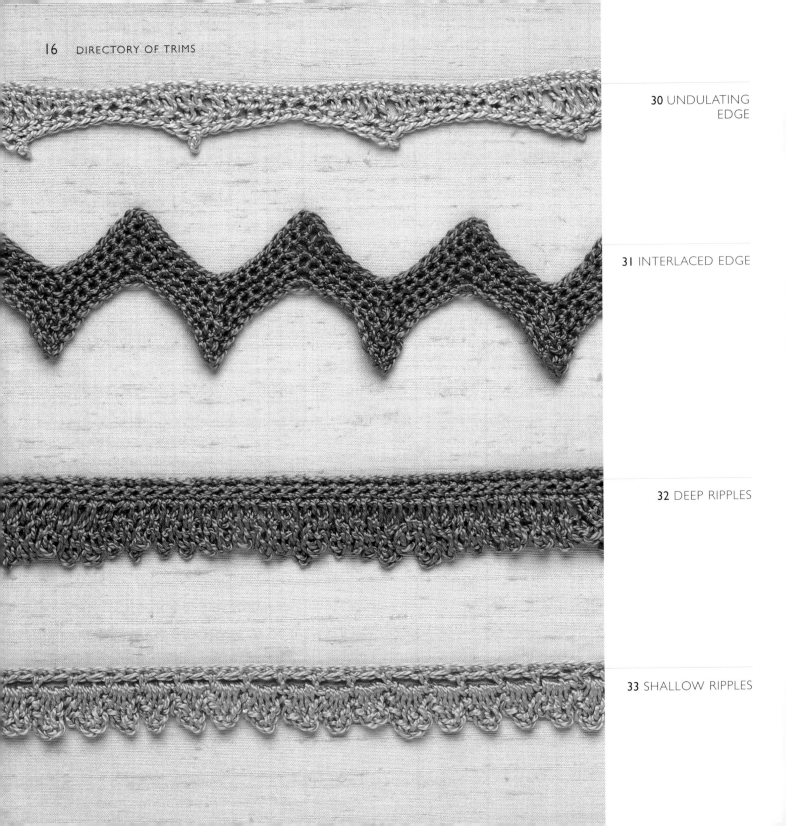

30 UNDULATING EDGE

31 INTERLACED EDGE

32 DEEP RIPPLES

33 SHALLOW RIPPLES

34 FRILLY EDGE

35 SURFACE BLOCKS

36 PARALLEL LINES

37 FRILLED EDGING

FRINGES

A crocheted fringe is a fun way to add a touch of glamour and movement to a plain knitted or crocheted garment. Here you'll find fringes in a range of yarn types from fine and delicate to thick and chunky. There are also examples using novelty yarns, beads and sequins in ways that won't overwhelm the look of the original piece.

TO MAKE:

For fringe patterns, see pages 58–66

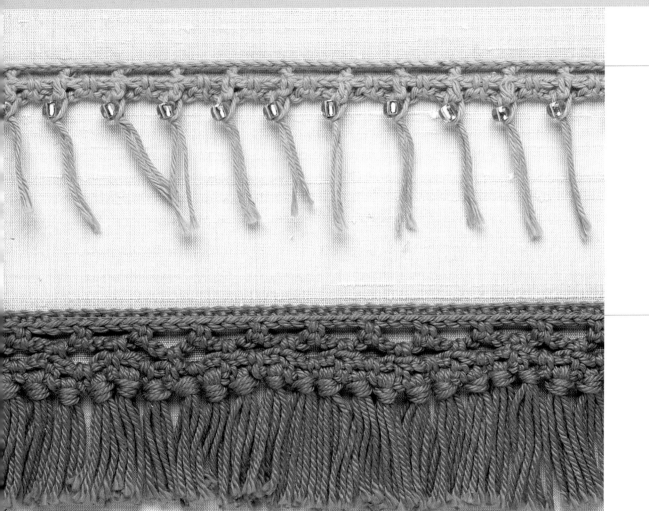

38 BEADED FILET FRINGE

39 TRIPLE LOOP FRINGE

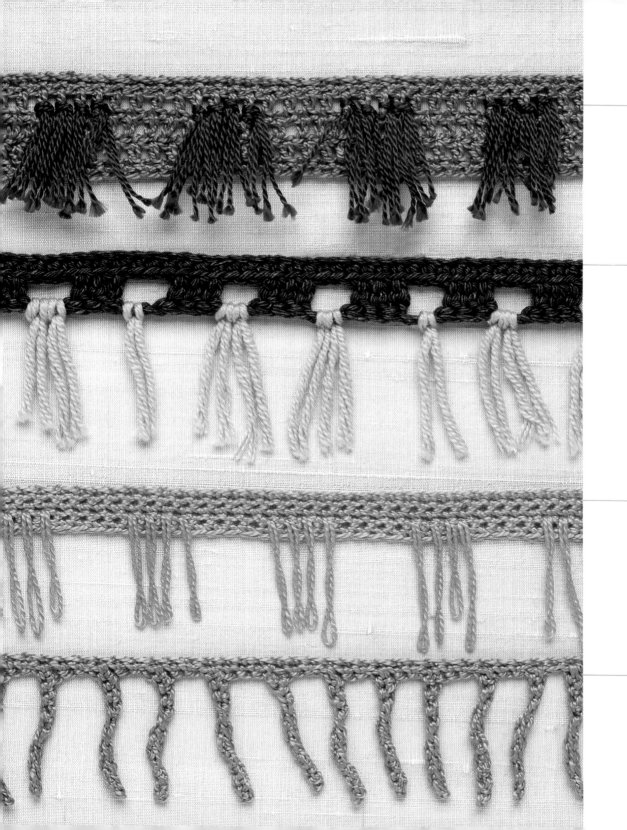

40 BLOCK FRINGE

41 OPEN BLOCK
FRINGE

42 RANDOM
FRINGE

43 DOUBLE
CROCHET FRINGE

44 TWISTED FRINGE

45 CURLICUE
FRINGE

46 CORKSCREW
FRINGE

47 SUPER SEQUINS

48 RINGLET FRINGE

49 SLIP FRINGE

50 TWISTED BULLIONS

51 ONLY BEADS

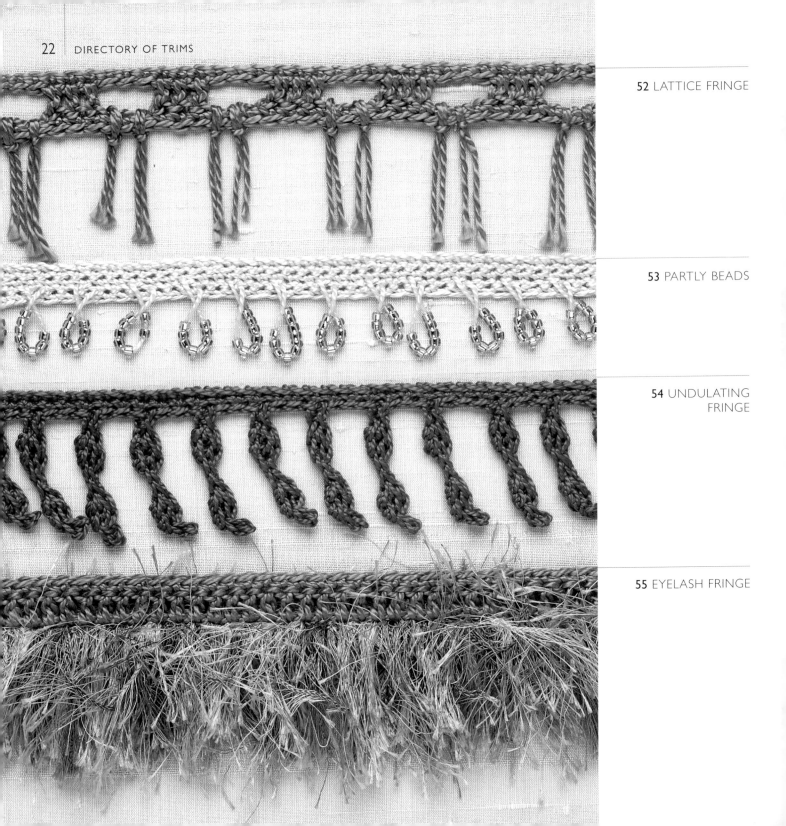

52 LATTICE FRINGE

53 PARTLY BEADS

54 UNDULATING
FRINGE

55 EYELASH FRINGE

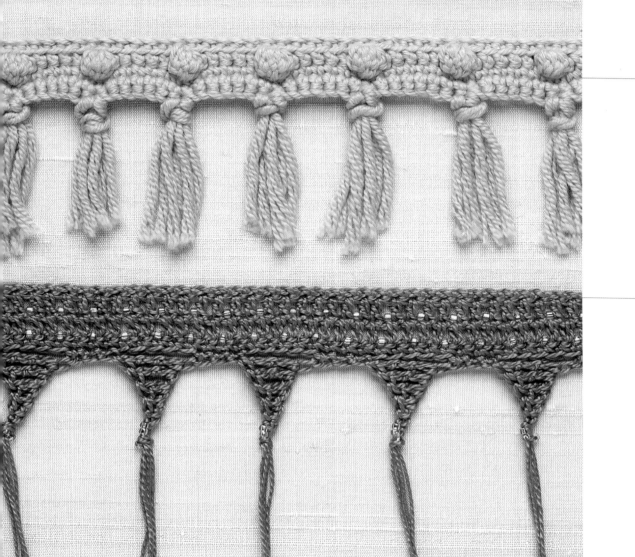

56 POPCORN
FRINGE

57 BEADED
TRIANGLES

58 BEADED LOOPS

59 CHEVRON FRINGE

60 BEADED
CHEVRONS FRINGE

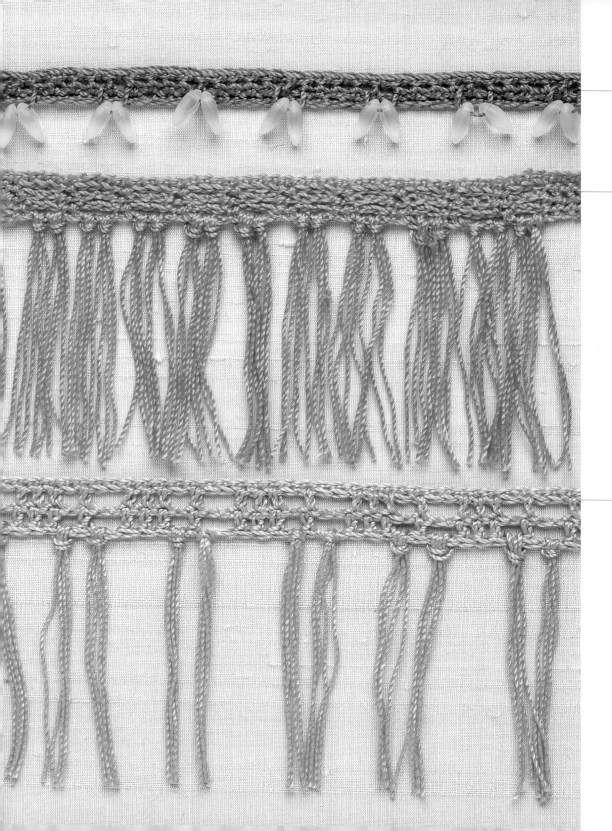

61 PEARL LEAF
FRINGE

62 DOUBLE MESH
FRINGE

63 GRANNY FRINGE

BRAIDS

Whether you want a braid with bobbles, waves, sequins, beads, chevrons or stripes there's a huge range to choose from in this section. Versatile braids can be delicately stitched to a garment or firmly glued to soft furnishings, adding fine and detailed decoration.

TO MAKE:

For braid patterns, see pages 67–73

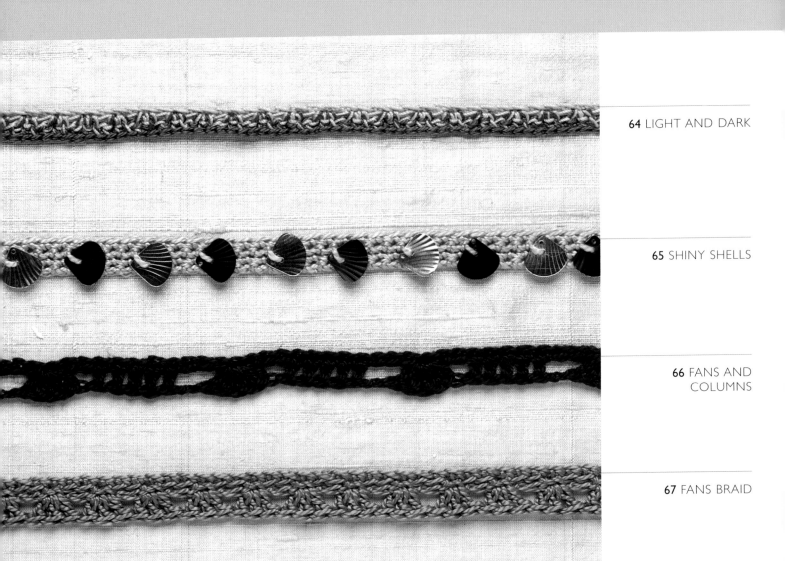

64 LIGHT AND DARK

65 SHINY SHELLS

66 FANS AND COLUMNS

67 FANS BRAID

68 SOFT CENTRE

69 BLOCKS BRAID

70 MOVING BLOCKS

71 FINE BLOCKS

72 LAZY FANS

73 WAVES BRAID

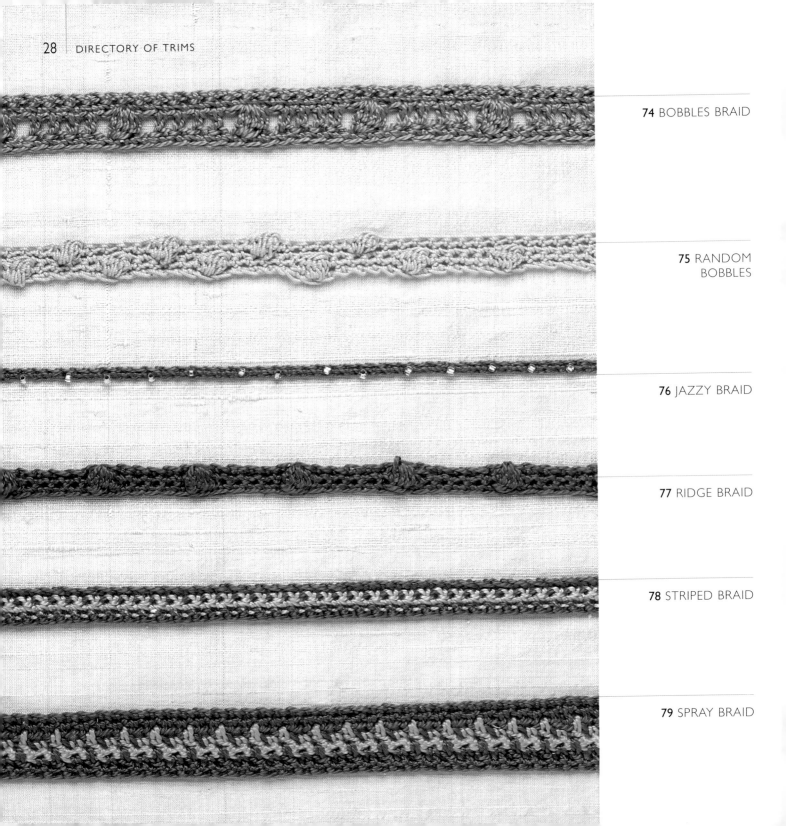

74 BOBBLES BRAID

75 RANDOM BOBBLES

76 JAZZY BRAID

77 RIDGE BRAID

78 STRIPED BRAID

79 SPRAY BRAID

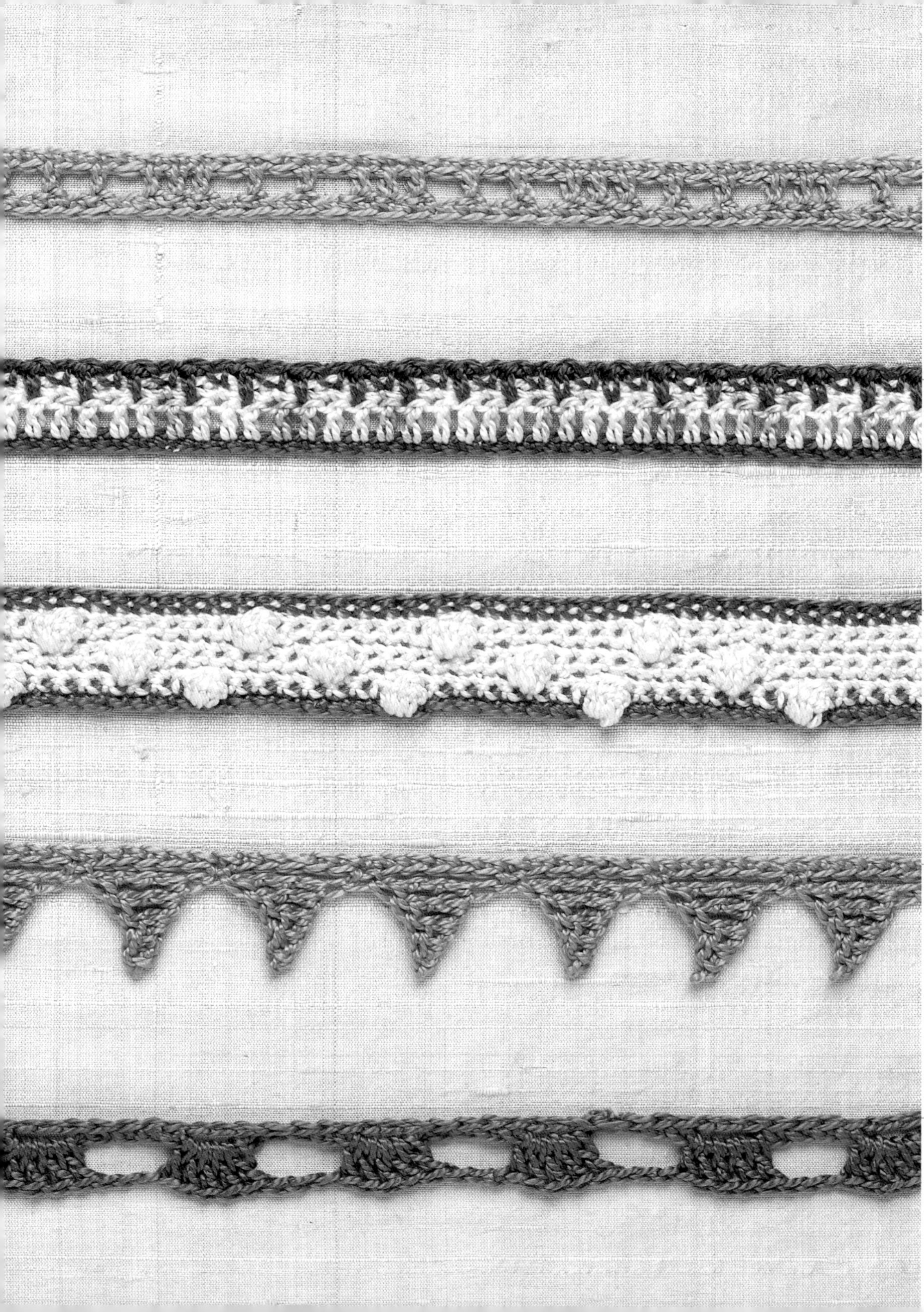

80 EYELET BRAID

81 LAYER BRAID

82 BOBBLE STEPS

83 PYRAMIDS BRAID

84 SHEATHS BRAID

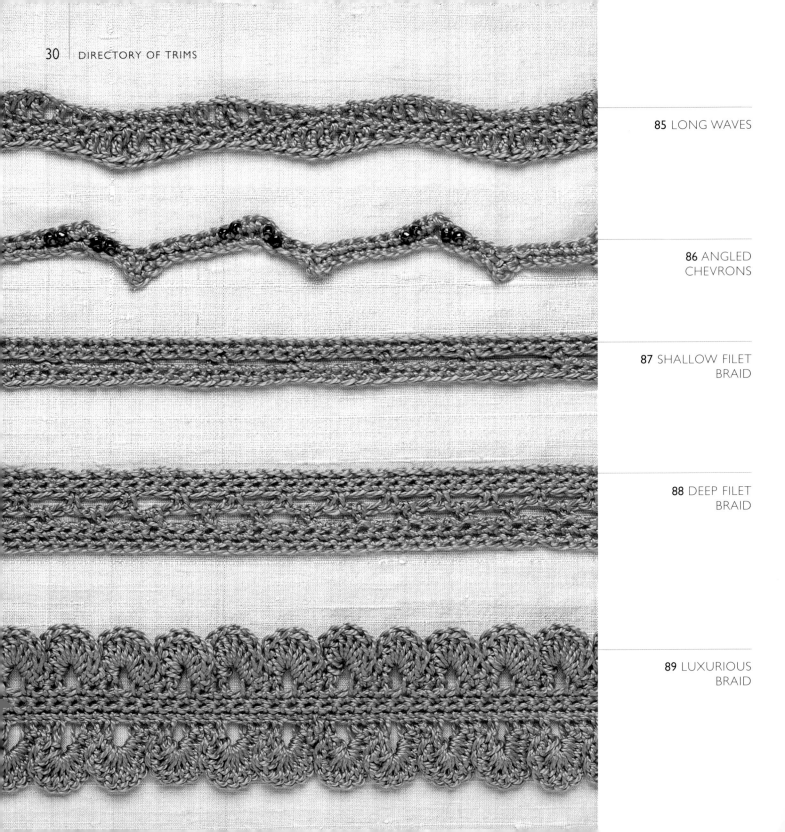

85 LONG WAVES

86 ANGLED
CHEVRONS

87 SHALLOW FILET
BRAID

88 DEEP FILET
BRAID

89 LUXURIOUS
BRAID

MOTIFS

Fashionable and versatile, crocheted motifs can be attached to a brooch back to pin to your favourite jacket or hat, sewn to a silky cushion, or added to a blank greetings card for a special occasion. Incorporating many themes, including flowers, leaves and snowflakes, these exciting decorations can take the form of simple silhouettes or three-dimensional, bead-embellished bouquets.

TO MAKE:

For motif patterns, see pages 74–86

90 SUN DAISY

93 CLOVER

91 GOLDEN PANSY

94 IRISH SHAMROCK

92 SUNBURST

95 LINKED PETALS

96 SUNSHINE

97 ENGLISH ROSE

98 IRISH LEAF

99 PRINCELY PETALS

100 FAN CIRCLE

101 SILHOUETTE CLOVER

102 WESTERN MOTIF

103 LAYERED ROSE

104 ELEGANT ROSE

105 FLOWER
SILHOUETTE

106 EASTERN MOTIF

107 INTRICATE
PETALS

108 ELEGANT
PETALS

109 SHELL FLOWER

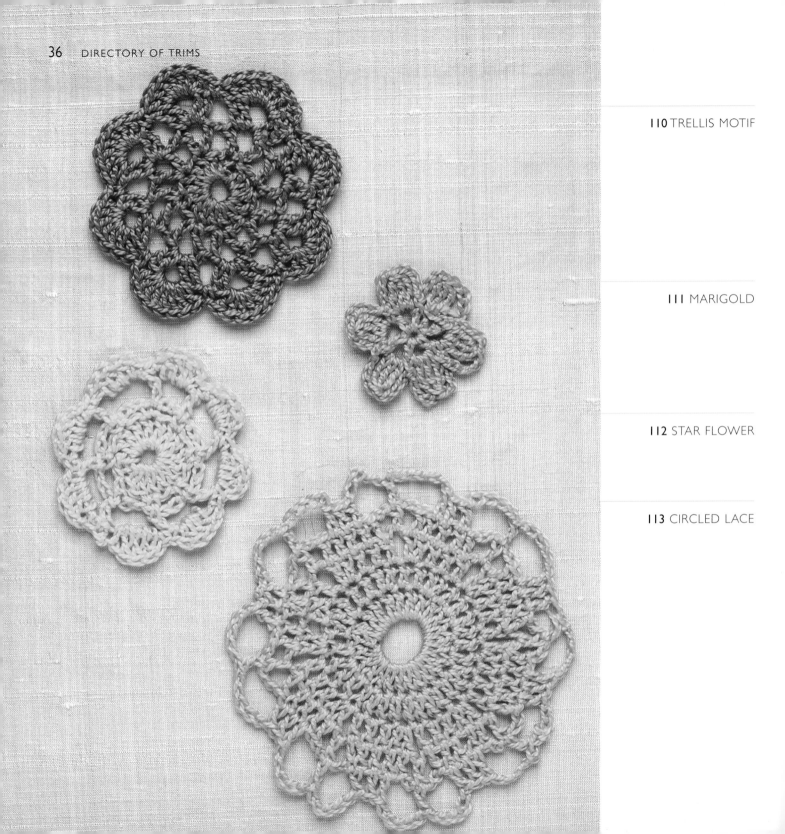

110 TRELLIS MOTIF

111 MARIGOLD

112 STAR FLOWER

113 CIRCLED LACE

114 FRAMED FLOWER

115 SQUARE FRAMED
CIRCLES

116 PINWHEEL

117 CHRYSANTHEMUM

118 CHAIN FLOWER

119 GOLDEN LEAF

120 LAZY FROG

122 CONICAL SHELL

123 PEARL ROSE

124 SNOWFLAKE

ACCESSORIES

The accessories included in this directory are decorative but functional crocheted items, that will not only add visual interest to a garment but also serve a purpose. On the next few pages you'll find chunky crochet-covered buttons, decorative buttonholes, floral collars, lacy insertions and tasselled and beaded belt ties.

TO MAKE:

For accessory patterns, see pages 87–97

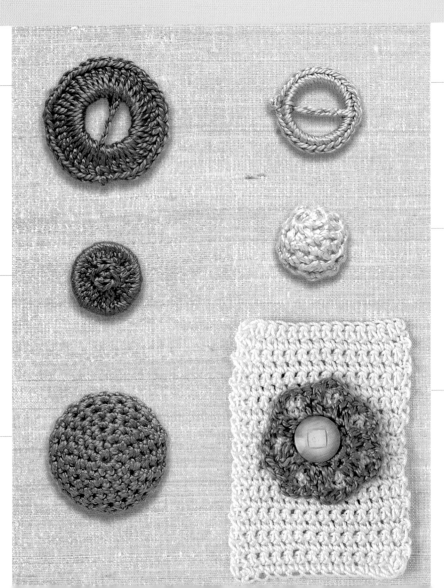

125 RING BUTTON 1

126 RING BUTTON 2

128 BALL BUTTON

127 RING BUTTON 3

130 FLORAL BUTTONHOLE

129 COVERED BUTTON

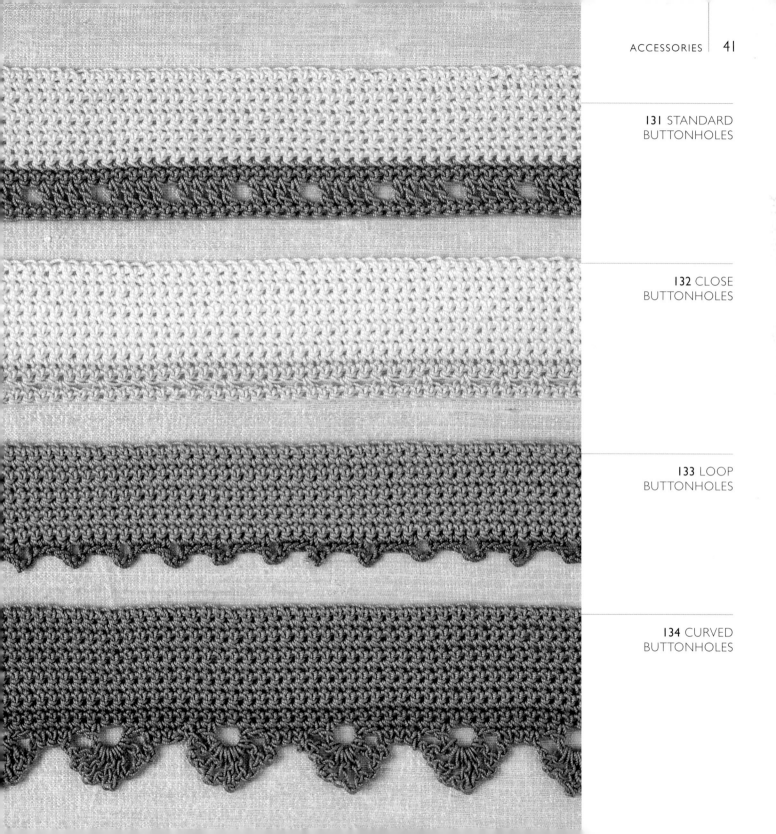

131 STANDARD
BUTTONHOLES

132 CLOSE
BUTTONHOLES

133 LOOP
BUTTONHOLES

134 CURVED
BUTTONHOLES

135 LOOPED PICOT
BUTTONHOLES

136 PICOT
BUTTONHOLES

137 TEXTURED
RUFFLE

138 DIAMONDS
INSERTION

139 DECORATIVE CUFF

140 COLUMNS INSERTION

141 SPIKED COLUMNS INSERTION

142 MINI CIRCLES INSERTION

143 BASIC COLLAR

144 LACE COLLAR

145 INTRICATE LACE
COLLAR

146 FAN COLLAR

147 PICOT COLLAR

148 RINGS BELT

149 DOUBLE RINGS BELT

150 BEADED BELT TIE

TECHNICAL DATA

This chapter contains all the information you need to make the
trims in the directory. Each crochet pattern is accompanied by a list
of the materials needed, and a page reference and trim number to
guide you to its position in the directory. There is also a detailed
photograph of the trim so that you can see the stitches.

EDGINGS

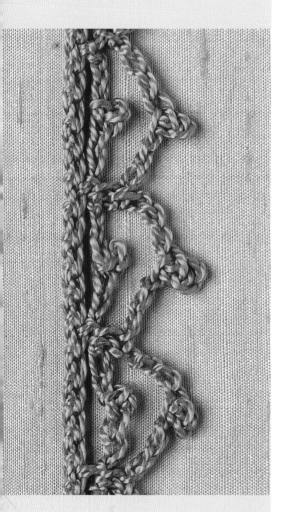

SEE ALSO

Standard crochet abbreviations,
page 125
Refresher course,
pages 110–125

 SHELL EDGE
Directory view, page 10

Skill level: Beginner/easy

 Worked in cotton perle in two colours: A and B

METHOD

Using colour A, make a foundation chain of the required length, or work row 1 directly into the item to be trimmed with right side facing.
(multiple of 6 stitches + 1)
Row 1: (A) 1 ch, 1 dc in each st or position to end, turn.
Row 2: (A) As row 1.
Row 3: (A) As row 1. Fasten off.
Row 4: Join in colour B. 1 ch, *miss 2 dc, 5 tr in next dc, miss 2 sts, 1 dc in next st, rep from * to end. Fasten off.

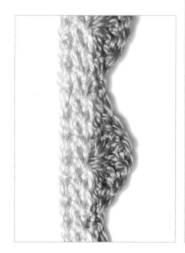

 SCALLOP EDGE
Directory view, page 10

Skill level: Beginner/easy

 Cotton perle

METHOD

Make a foundation chain of the required length, or work row 1 directly into the item to be trimmed with right side facing.
(multiple of 3 stitches + 1)
Row 1: 3 ch, 1 tr in each st to end, turn.
Row 2: 1 ch, *2 ch, miss 2 sts, 1 dc in next st, rep from * to end, turn.
Row 3: 1 ch, *(1 dc, 1 htr, 1 tr, 1 dtr, 1 tr, 1 htr, 1 dc) in 2-ch sp, rep from * to end. Fasten off.

GLITZY EDGE
Directory view, page 10

Skill level: Beginner/easy

 Cotton perle

 25 mm circular holographic sequins

METHOD

Thread the sequins onto the yarn before beginning.
Make a foundation chain of the required length, or work row 1 directly into the item to be trimmed with right side facing.
(multiple of 4 stitches + 1)
Row 1: 1 ch, 1 dc in each st to end, turn.
Row 2: As row 1.
Row 3: 3 ch, 1 tr in each st to end, turn.
Row 4: 3 ch, *3 tr, pull down first sequin into next tr, rep from * to end. Fasten off.

 LARGE PICOT EDGE
Directory view, page 11

Skill level: Beginner/easy

 Cotton perle

METHOD

Make a foundation chain of the required length, or work row 1 directly into the item to be trimmed with right side facing.
(multiple of 3 stitches + 1)
Row 1: 1 ch, 1 dc in each st to end, turn.
Row 2: As row 1.
Row 3: 1 ch, *1 dc, 5 ch, 1 ss in first of these 5 ch, miss 1 st, 1 dc, rep from * to end. Fasten off.

 BLOCK EDGE
Directory view, page 11

Skill level: Intermediate

 Cotton perle

METHOD

Make a foundation chain of the required length, or work row 1 directly into the item to be trimmed with right side facing.
(multiple of 4 stitches + 1)
Row 1: 1 ch, 1 dc in each st to end, turn.
Row 2: As row 1.
Row 3: 4 ch, *miss 3 sts, 1 dtr in next st, 3 ch, 4 tr around stem of dtr just worked, rep from * to end. Fasten off.

 SHELLS AND BEADS
Directory view, page 11

Skill level: Intermediate

 DK (double knitting)

 5 mm glass seed beads

METHOD

Thread the beads onto the yarn before beginning.
Make a foundation chain of the required length, or work row 1 directly into the item to be trimmed with right side facing.
(multiple of 6 stitches + 1)
Row 1: 1 ch, 1 dc in 2nd ch from hook, *3 ch, miss 3 sts, 3 dc, rep from * to end, turn.
Row 2: 1 ch, 1 dc, miss 1 st *(5 tr in 3-ch sp – working bead into 3rd of these tr), miss 1 st, 1 dc in next st, miss 1 st, rep from * to end. Fasten off.

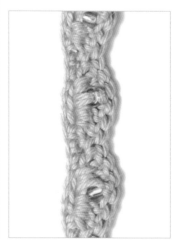

7 REGULAR WAVES

Directory view, page 11

Skill level: Beginner/easy

 Cotton perle

METHOD

Make a foundation chain of the required length, or work row 1 directly into the item to be trimmed with right side facing. (multiple of 10 stitches + 1)
Row 1: 1 ch, 1 dc in 2nd ch from hook, *5 tr, 5 dc, rep from * to end, turn.
Row 2: 1 ch, 4 dc, 5 tr, * 5 dc, 5 tr, rep from * to last st, 1 dc. Fasten off.

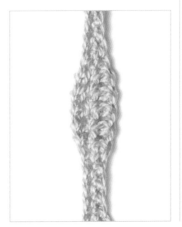

8 FUZZY EDGE

Directory view, page 11

Skill level: Beginner/easy

 Worked in two yarns: cotton perle (smooth) and DK eyelash yarn (fuzzy)

METHOD

Using the smooth yarn, make a foundation chain of the required length, or work row 1 directly into the item to be trimmed with right side facing. (any number of stitches)
Row 1: (smooth) 1 ch, 1 dc in each chain to end, turn.
Row 2: (smooth) 3 ch, 1 tr in each st to end. Fasten off.
Row 3: (fuzzy) As row 1.
Row 4: (fuzzy) As row 1. Fasten off.

9 ARCADE EDGE

Directory view, page 11

Skill level: Beginner/easy

 Cotton perle

METHOD

Make a foundation chain of the required length, or work row 1 directly into the item to be trimmed with right side facing. (multiple of 6 stitches + 3)
Row 1: 1 ch, 1 dc in each st to end, turn.
Row 2: 1 ch, 2 dc, *3 ch, miss 3 sts, 3 dc, rep from * to end, turn.
Row 3: 1 ch, 1 dc, *5 tr in 3-ch sp, miss 1 st, 1 dc, miss 1 st, rep from * to end. Fasten off.

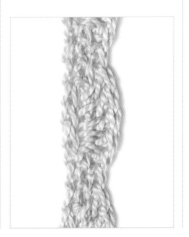

10 SHARP CHEVRONS

Directory view, page 12

Skill level: Intermediate

 Cotton perle

METHOD

Make a foundation chain of the required length, or work row 1 directly into the item to be trimmed with right side facing. (multiple of 16 stitches)
Row 1: 3 ch, 1 tr in 4th ch from hook, *4 tr, (tr3tog) twice, 4 tr, (3 tr in next st) twice, rep from * to end, omitting last 3 tr of final repeat. Fasten off.

LATTICE CHEVRONS

Directory view, page 12

Skill level: Intermediate

 Cotton perle

METHOD

Make a foundation chain of the required length, or work row 1 directly into the item to be trimmed with right side facing. (multiple of 20 stitches + 1)

Row 1: 4 ch, 1 tr in 5th ch from hook, *(1 ch, miss 1 st, 1 tr) 3 times, 1 ch, miss 1 st, (tr2tog) working 1st tr in next st, miss 3 ch and 2nd tr in next st), (1 ch, miss 1 st, 1 tr in next st) 3 times, 1 ch, miss 1 st, (1 tr, 3 ch, 1 tr in next st), rep from * to end, turn.

Row 2: 6 ch, 1 tr in 3-ch loop, *6 tr, (tr2tog) working 1st tr in next st, miss 3 st and 2nd tr in next st), 6 tr, (1 tr, 3 ch, 1 tr) in 3-ch sp, rep from * to end. Fasten off.

 ## SOFT EDGE

Directory view, page 12

Skill level: Beginner/easy

 Worked in two yarns: cotton perle (smooth) and mohair

METHOD

Using the smooth yarn, make a foundation chain of the required length, or work row 1 directly into the item to be trimmed with right side facing. (odd number of stitches)

Row 1: (smooth) 1 ch, 1 dc in each st to end. Fasten off, turn.

Row 2: (mohair) 3 ch, 1 tr in same st, *miss 1 st, 2 tr in next st, rep from * to end. Fasten off.

 ## ARCHES EDGE

Directory view, page 12

Skill level: Beginner/easy

 Variegated cotton perle

METHOD

Make a foundation chain of the required length, or work row 1 directly into the item to be trimmed with right side facing. (multiple of 5 stitches + 3)

Row 1: 1 ch, 1 dc in each st to end, turn.

Row 2: 1 ch, *2 dc, 5 ch, miss 2 sts, 3 dc, rep from * to end, turn.

Row 3: As row 1. Fasten off.

PICOT ARCHES

Directory view, page 12

Skill level: Intermediate

Cotton perle

METHOD

Notes: picot = 3 ch, sl st into 3rd ch from hook.

Make a foundation chain of the required length, or work row 1 directly into the item to be trimmed with right side facing. (multiple of 6 stitches)

Row 1: 1 ch, 1 dc in each st to end, turn.

Row 2: 1 ch, 1 dc in first st, *5 ch, miss 4 sts, 1 dc in next st, 3 picots, 1 dc in next st, rep from * to last 5 sts, 5 ch, miss 4 sts, 1 dc in last st, turn.

Row 3: 3 ch, 1 dc in 5-ch arch, *8 ch, 1 dc in 5-ch arch, rep from * to last 5-ch arch, 2 ch, 1 dc in last st, turn.

Row 4: 1 ch, miss 2-ch arch, 1 dc in next dc, *11 dc in 8-ch arch, 1 dc in next st, rep from * to end. Fasten off.

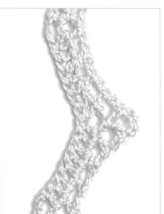

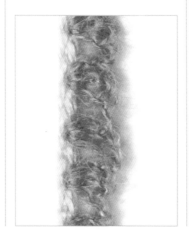

RHYTHMIC EDGE
Directory view, page 13

Skill level: Beginner/easy

 Cotton perle

METHOD

Make a foundation chain of the required length, or work row 1 directly into the item to be trimmed with right side facing. (multiple of 8 stitches + 1)
Row 1: 1 ch, 1 dc in each st to end, turn.
Row 2: As row 1.
Row 3: 1 ch, *6 dc, miss 2 dc, 6 tr, rep from * to end, turn.
Row 4: As row 1. Fasten off.

 BEADED WAVES
Directory view, page 13

Skill level: Intermediate

 Cotton perle

3 mm glass seed beads

METHOD

Thread the beads onto the yarn before beginning.
Make a foundation chain of the required length, or work row 1 directly into the item to be trimmed with right side facing. (odd number of stitches)
Row 1: 1 ch, 1 dc in each st to end, turn.
Row 2: 3 ch, *bring down a bead to work into next tr, 1 tr, rep from * to end
Row 3: 1 ch, *1 htr, 1 dc, rep from * to end. Fasten off.

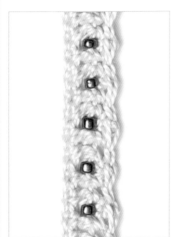

 SCALLOPED ARCHES
Directory view, page 13

Skill level: Beginner/easy

 Cotton perle

METHOD

Make a foundation chain of the required length, or work row 1 directly into the item to be trimmed with right side facing. (multiple of 4 stitches + 1)
Row 1: 1 ch, 1 dc in each st to end, turn.
Row 2: 1 ch, *5 ch, miss 3 sts, 1 dc into next st, rep * to end, turn.
Row 3: 1 ch, *7 ch, miss 5-ch loop, 1 dc into next st, rep from * to end. Fasten off.

ARCH AND PICOT EDGE
Directory view, page 13

Skill level: Intermediate

Cotton perle

METHOD

Make a foundation chain of the required length, or work row 1 directly into the item to be trimmed with right side facing. (multiple of 5 stitches + 1)
Row 1: 1 ch, 1 dc in each st to end, turn.
Row 2: 1 ch, *5 ch, sl st into 3rd ch from hook, 3 ch, miss 4 sts, 1 dc in next st, rep from * to end, turn.
Row 3: 1 ch, *6 ch, sl st into 3rd ch from hook, 4 ch, miss 4 sts, 1 dc in next st, rep from * to end. Fasten off.

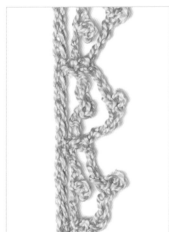

SHALLOW SCALLOPS
Directory view, page 13

Skill level: Intermediate

 Worked in cotton perle in two colours: A and B

METHOD

Using colour A, make a foundation chain of the required length, or work row 1 directly into the item to be trimmed with right side facing. (multiple of 6 stitches + 2)
Row 1: (A) 1 ch, 1 dc in each st to end, turn.
Row 2: (A) 3 ch, 1 tr, *1 ch, miss 1 st, 2 tr; rep from * to end. Fasten off, turn.
Row 3: (B) *4 ch, 1 dc in next ch sp, rep from * to last ch sp, 2 ch, 1 dc in last st, turn.
Row 4: (B) 1 ch, 1 dc in 2-ch sp, *5 tr in next 4-ch sp, 1 dc in next 4-ch sp, rep from * to end. Fasten off.

 MESH ARCHES
Directory view, page 14

Skill level: Beginner/easy

 Cotton perle

METHOD

Make a foundation chain of the required length, or work row 1 directly into the item to be trimmed with right side facing. (multiple of 4 stitches + 1)
Row 1: 4 ch, 1 tr in 7th ch from hook, *1 ch, miss 1 st, 1 tr in next st, rep from * to end, turn.
Row 2: 1 ch, *5 ch, (miss 1 ch, 1 tr, 1 ch), 1 dc in next st, rep from * to end, turn.
Row 3: 1 ch, *7 dc in 5-ch arch, 1 dc in next st, rep from * to end. Fasten off.

 IRIS EDGE
Directory view, page 14

Skill level: Intermediate

 Cotton perle

METHOD

Make a foundation chain of the required length, or work row 1 directly into the item to be trimmed with right side facing. (multiple of 4 stitches + 1)
Row 1: 3 ch, (1 tr, 1 ch, 2 tr) in 4th ch from hook, *miss 3 ch, (2 tr, 1 ch, 2 tr) in next st, rep from * to end. Fasten off.

 BEADS AND DOUBLES
Directory view, page 14

Skill level: Intermediate

 Cotton perle

5 mm glass seed beads

METHOD

Thread the beads onto the yarn before beginning.
Make a foundation chain of the required length, or work row 1 directly into the item to be trimmed with right side facing. (multiple of 4 stitches + 3)
Row 1: 1 ch, 1 dc in each st to end, turn.
Row 2: 3 ch, 2 tr, *miss 1 dc, bring down bead work into next dc, 2 tr, rep from * to end, turn.
Row 3: As row 1. Fasten off.

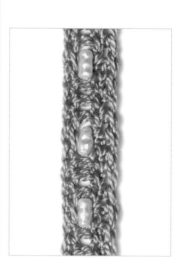

23 CHAIN ARCHES
Directory view, page 14

Skill level: Beginner/easy

 Cotton perle

METHOD

Make a foundation chain of the required length, or work row 1 directly into the item to be trimmed with right side facing. (odd number of stitches)
Row 1: 1 ch, 1 dc in each st to end, turn.
Row 2: As row 1.
Row 3: 1 ch, *3 ch, miss 1 st, 1 dc in next st, rep from * to end. Fasten off.

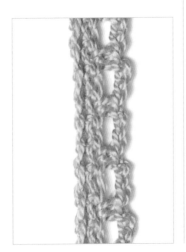

24 WAVES EDGE
Directory view, page 14

Skill level: Intermediate

 Cotton perle

METHOD

Make a foundation chain of the required length, or work row 1 directly into the item to be trimmed with right side facing. (multiple of 6 stitches + 3)
Row 1: 1 ch, 1 dc in each st to end, turn.
Row 2: As row 1.
Row 3: As row 1.
Row 4: 1 ch, 2 dc, *6 ch, miss 3 sts, 3 dc, rep from * to end, turn.
Row 5: 1 ch, 2 dc, *(3 dc, 1 htr, 1 tr, 1 htr, 3 dc) in 6-ch loop, 3 dc, rep from * to end. Fasten off.

25 LAYERED CHAINS
Directory view, page 15

Skill level: Intermediate

 Worked in cotton perle in three colours: A, B and C

METHOD

Using colour A, make a foundation chain of the required length, or work row 1 directly into the item to be trimmed with right side facing. (multiple of 3 stitches + 1)
Row 1: (A) 1 ch, 1 dc in each st to end, turn.
Row 2: (A) As row 1.
Row 3: (A) As row 1. Fasten off, turn.
Row 4: (B) 3 ch, 1 tr in first st, *5 ch, miss 2 sts, 1 tr in next st, rep from * to end. Fasten off, turn.
Row 5: Join in colour C to left of 1st tr in row 1 and work as row 4. Fasten off.

26 SIMPLY BEADS
Directory view, page 15

Skill level: Intermediate

 Cotton perle

 3 mm glass seed beads

METHOD

Thread the beads onto the yarn before beginning.
Make a foundation chain of the required length, or work row 1 directly into the item to be trimmed with right side facing. (multiple of 10 stitches + 1)
Row 1: 1 ch, 1 dc in each st to end, turn.
Row 2: 3 ch, *1 tr, bring down bead in next tr, rep from * to end, turn.
Row 3: As row 2.
Row 4: As row 1.
Row 5: 1 ch, *bring down bead in next dc, 4 dc, rep from * to end. Fasten off.

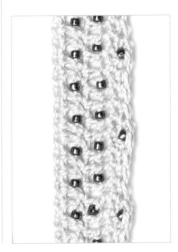

27 FLORAL EDGE
Directory view, page 15

Skill level: Intermediate

 Cotton perle

METHOD

Make a foundation chain of the required length, or work row 1 directly into the item to be trimmed with right side facing. (multiple of 4 stitches + 1)
Row 1: 3 ch, (1 tr, 1 ch, 2 tr) in same st, *miss 3 ch, (2 tr, 1 ch, 2 tr) in next st, rep from * to end, turn.
Row 2: 3 ch, (1 tr, 1 ch, 2 tr) in first ch sp, (2 tr, 1 ch, 2 tr) in each ch sp to end. Fasten off.

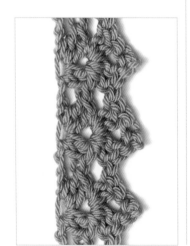

28 POSY EDGE
Directory view, page 15

Skill level: Intermediate

 Cotton perle

METHOD

There is no foundation chain for this edging.
Row 1: 4 ch, 1 tr in 4th ch from hook (centre ring made), (3 ch, 2 tr into ring, 3 ch, 1 sl st in ring) 3 times (3 petals made = 1 motif), *11 ch, 1 tr into 4th ch from hook, 3 ch, 1 tr in ring, 1 sl st between 2 tr of last petal made, 1 tr into ring, 3 ch, 1 sl st in ring, (3 ch, 2 tr in ring, 3 ch, 1 sl st in ring) twice, rep from * to length required. Fasten off.

29 IRIS STITCH EDGE
Directory view, page 15

Skill level: Challenging/complex

 Cotton perle

METHOD

Make a foundation chain of the required length, or work row 1 directly into the item to be trimmed with right side facing. (multiple of 4 stitches + 1)
Row 1: 4 ch, 3 tr in 5th ch from hook, *miss 3 ch, (1 tr, 3 ch, 3 tr) in next st, rep from * to end. Fasten off.

30 UNDULATING EDGE
Directory view, page 16

Skill level: Intermediate

 Cotton perle

METHOD

Notes: Picot = 3 ch, sl st into 3rd ch from hook.
Make a foundation chain of the required length, or work row 1 directly into the item to be trimmed with right side facing. (multiple of 12 + 3 stitches)
Row 1: 1 ch, 1 dc in each st or position to end, turn.
Row 2: 1 ch, 2 dc, *2 htr, 2 tr, 2 dtr, 2 tr, 2 htr, 2 tr, rep from * to end, turn.
Row 3: 1 ch, *1 dc in each of next 6 sts, picot between 2 dtr, 1 dc in each of next 6 sts, rep from * to last 2 sts, 2 dc. Fasten off.

31 ## INTERLACED EDGE
Directory view, page 16

Skill level: Intermediate

 Cotton perle

METHOD

Make a foundation chain of the required length, or work row 1 directly into the item to be trimmed with right side facing. (multiple of 16 stitches + 1)
Row 1: 1 ch, 2 dc in 2nd ch from hook, *1 dc in each of next 7 ch, miss 1 ch, 1 dc in each of next 7 ch, 3 dc in next ch, rep from * to end, omitting 1 tr at end of last rep, turn.
Row 2: 1 ch, 2 dc in first dc, *1 dc in each of next 7 dc, miss 2 dc, 1 dc in each of next 7 dc, 3 dc in next dc, rep from * to end omitting 1 tr at end of last rep.
Rep row 2 for required length.
Fasten off.

 32 ## DEEP RIPPLES
Directory view, page 16

Skill level: Beginner/easy

 Cotton perle

METHOD

Make a foundation chain of the required length, or work row 1 directly into the item to be trimmed with right side facing. (any number of stitches)
Row 1: 1 ch, 1 dc in each st to end, turn.
Row 2: As row 1.
Row 3: As row 1.
Row 4: 1 ch, 1 dc in first st, 5 ch, *(1 dc, 5 ch) in next st, rep from * to end, omitting last 5 ch.
Fasten off.

 33 ## SHALLOW RIPPLES
Directory view, page 16

Skill level: Beginner/easy

 Cotton perle

METHOD

Make a foundation chain of the required length, or work row 1 directly into the item to be trimmed with right side facing. (even number of stitches)
Row 1: 1 ch, 1 dc in each ch or position to end, turn.
Row 2: 1 ch, *1 dc, 2 ch, miss 1 ch, rep from * to end, omitting last 2 ch, turn.
Row 3: 1 ch, *(1 dc, 1 ch, 1 htr, 1 ch, 1 tr, 1 ch, 1 htr, 1 ch, 1 dc) in 2-ch loop, rep from * to end.
Fasten off.

 34 ## FRILLY EDGE
Directory view, page 17

Skill level: Beginner/easy

 Cotton perle

METHOD

Make a foundation chain of the required length, or work row 1 directly into the item to be trimmed with right side facing. (any number of stitches)
Row 1: 1 ch, 1 dc in each ch to end, turn.
Row 2: As row 1.
Row 3: 3 ch, 1 tr in each dc to end, turn.
Row 4: 2 ch, (3 tr, 1 ch) in each tr to end. Omit 1 ch at end of row. Fasten off.

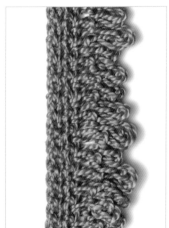

35 SURFACE BLOCKS
Directory view, page 17

Skill level: Beginner/easy

 Worked in cotton perle in two colours: A and B

METHOD

Make a foundation chain of the required length, or work row 1 directly into the item to be trimmed with right side facing. (multiple of 7 stitches + 1)
Row 1: 3 ch, 1 tr in 4th ch from hook, 1 tr in each ch to end, turn.
Rows 2–6: 1 ch, 1 dc into each st to end, turn. Fasten off.
Raised stitch: Using a contrasting colour yarn, starting at the tr row, holding the crochet hook on top of the work with the incoming yarn held in the normal way, under the fabric, work *4 ch across middle of tr row, 2 ch down, 4 ch across, 2 ch up, rep from * to end. Fasten off.

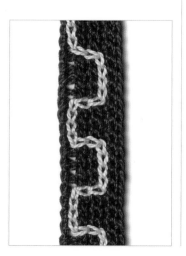

36 PARALLEL LINES
Directory view, page 17

Skill level: Beginner/easy

 Worked in cotton perle in three colours

METHOD

Make a foundation chain of the required length, or work row 1 directly into the item to be trimmed with right side facing. (any number of stitches)
Row 1: 3 ch, 1 tr in 4th ch from hook, 1 tr in each ch to end, turn.
Rows 2–5: 1 ch, 1 dc into each st to end, turn.
Row 6: 3 ch, 1 tr in 4th ch from hook, 1 tr in each ch to end, turn.
Fasten off.
Raised stitch: Using a contrasting colour yarn, starting at the top edge, holding the crochet hook on top of the work with the incoming yarn held in the normal way, but under the edging, make a sl st onto hook, work a straight line to end.
Using a second contrasting yarn, working in the same way, sl st another line next to the first, fasten off.

37 FRILLED EDGING
Directory view, page 17

Skill level: Intermediate

 Cotton perle

METHOD

Make a foundation chain of the required length, or work row 1 directly into the item to be trimmed with right side facing. (even number of stitches)
Row 1: 1 ch, 1 dc in each ch to end, turn.
Row 2: *5 ch, miss next st, sl st into next st, rep from * to end, turn.
Row 3: 1 ch, (1 dc, [3 ch, 1 dc] 5 times) in each 1-ch sp to end. Fasten off.

FRINGES

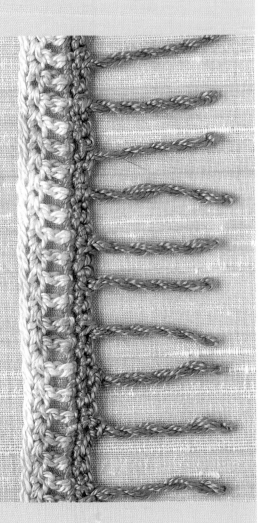

SEE ALSO

Standard crochet abbreviations, page 125
Refresher course, pages 110–125

38 BEADED FILET FRINGE
Directory view, page 18

Skill level: Beginner/easy

 Double knitting (DK weight)

5 mm glass seed beads

METHOD

Make a foundation chain of the required length, or work row 1 directly into the item to be trimmed with right side facing.
(multiple of 4 stitches + 1)
Row 1: 5 ch, 1 tr in 10th ch from hook, *3 ch, miss 3 sts, 1 tr in next st, rep from * to end, turn.
Row 2: 1 ch, *2 ch, 1 dc in 3 ch sp, 2 ch, 1 tr in next tr, rep from * to end. Fasten off.
Fringe: Basic fringe pattern, threading a bead over the loop (double thickness of yarn), attach as described on page 119, to trs on last row to end. Fasten off.

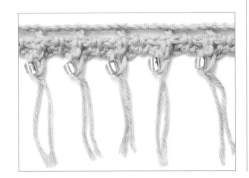

39 TRIPLE LOOP FRINGE
Directory view, page 18

Skill level: Intermediate

 Double knitting (DK weight)

METHOD

Make a foundation chain of the required length, or work row 1 directly into the item to be trimmed with right side facing.
(multiple of 4 stitches + 1)
Row 1: 1 ch, 1 dc in each ch to end, turn.
Row 2: 1 ch, *5 ch, miss 3 sts, 1 tr in back loop only of next st, rep from * to end, turn.
Row 3: 3 ch, *1 dc, 5 ch, 1 dc in 5-ch loop, rep from * to last loop, 2 ch, 1 dc in last st, turn.
Row 4: 2 ch, 1 dc in 2-ch loop, *2 ch, 1 dc in 5-ch loop, 2 ch, miss 1 dc, 1 dc in next dc, rep from * to last loop, 2 ch, 1 dc in last st. Fasten off.
Fringe: Make a basic fringe using three lengths of yarn in each 2-chain space, giving a delicate style.

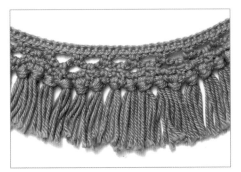

40 BLOCK FRINGE
Directory view, page 19

Skill level: Intermediate

 Worked in cotton perle in two colours

METHOD

Make a foundation chain of the required length, or work row 1 directly into the item to be trimmed with right side facing.
(multiple of 8 stitches + 1)
Row 1: 1 ch, 1 dc in each st to end, turn.
Row 2: As row 1.
Row 3: 3 ch, *1 tr in each st to end, turn.
Row 4: As row 3.
Row 5: As row 3.
Row 6: As row 1. Fasten off.
Fringe: Fold two lengths of a contrasting yarn and knot around a tr on row 2, add another three fringes in the same way, miss the next 4 tr, repeat this pattern across the row. You could also work fringes on 2, 3 or 4 consecutive rows for a denser look.

41 OPEN BLOCK FRINGE
Directory view, page 19

Skill level: Beginner/easy

 Worked in double knitting (DK weight) in two colours

METHOD

Make a foundation chain of the required length, or work row 1 directly into the item to be trimmed with right side facing.
(multiple of 6 stitches + 1)
Row 1: 1 ch, 1 dc in each chain to end, turn.
Row 2: 3 ch, *3 ch, miss 3 sts, 3 tr, rep from * to end. Fasten off.
Fringe: Using a single strand of contrasting yarn, *knot one piece in the first 3-chain space, two separate lengths in the next 3-chain space, repeat from * to end.

42 RANDOM FRINGE
Directory view, page 19

Skill level: Intermediate

 Worked in cotton perle in two colours

METHOD

Notes: Loop st: the loops will appear on the wrong side of the fabric as the loops are formed at the back of the fabric. Work the loop stitch as follows:
1. Insert hook into the st below, as usual. Using a finger of the free hand, pull up the yarn to form a loop of the required size. Pick up both strands of the loop and draw them through.
2. Wrap the yarn over the hook.
3. Draw the yarn through all 3 loops.
If the fringe loops hang the wrong way, straighten them by pinning and steaming in place.

Make a foundation chain of the required length, or work row 1 directly into the item to be trimmed with right side facing. (multiple of 8 stitches + 1) (To ensure that this fringe is on the correct side for your project, repeat row 1 if necessary.)
Row 1: 1 ch, 1 dc in each chain to end, turn.
Rows 2–3: As row 1.
Row 4: 1 ch, *1 loop st in each of next 4 sts, 1 dc in each of next 4 sts, rep from * to end, turn.
Row 5: As row 1. Fasten off.

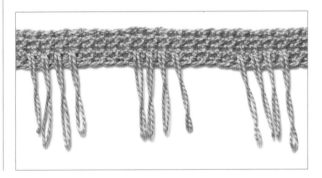

43 DOUBLE CROCHET FRINGE
Directory view, page 19

Skill level: Beginner/easy

 Cotton perle

METHOD

Make a foundation chain of the required length, or work row 1 directly into the item to be trimmed with right side facing.
(multiple of 3 stitches + 1)
Row 1: 1 ch, 1 dc in each ch to end, turn.
Row 2: 1 ch, *2 dc, 8 ch for fringe, 1 dc in 2nd ch from hook, 6 dc into fringe ch, 1 sl st in last dc worked on heading of fringe, 1 dc. Fasten off.

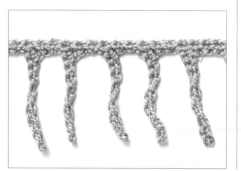

44 TWISTED FRINGE
Directory view, page 20

Skill level: Challenging/complex

 Worked in cotton perle in two colours: multicoloured yarn and plain yarn

METHOD

Using the multicoloured yarn make a foundation chain of the required length or work row 1 directly into the item to be trimmed with right side facing.
(multiple of 3 stitches + 1)
Row 1: (multicoloured yarn) 1 ch, 1 dc in each ch to end. Fasten off, turn.
Row 2: (multicoloured yarn) 3 ch, 1 tr in each dc to end, turn.
Row 3: (plain yarn) As row 1.
Row 4: (plain yarn) 1 ch, *2 dc, (1 dc in next st, extend loop on hook to twice the required fringe length, with hook still in the loop twist 8 times, allow the loop to twist tog, 1 dc into same stitch), rep from * to last st, 1 dc, rep from * to end. Fasten off.

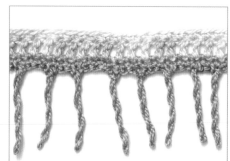

45 CURLICUE FRINGE
Directory view, page 20

Skill level: Challenging/complex

 Worked in cotton perle in two colours: A and B

METHOD

Using yarn A, make a foundation chain of the required length, or work row 1 directly into the item to be trimmed with right side facing.
(multiple of 4 stitches + 1)
Row 1: (A) 1 ch, 1 dc in each ch to end, turn.
Row 2: (A) 2 ch, 1 htr in each st to end, turn.
Row 3: (A) As row 2. Fasten off, turn.
Row 4: (B) 1 ch, *3 dc, ^9 ch, 4 dc in 3rd ch from hook, (4 tr in next ch) 6 times, 1 sl st in last dc worked on fringe header ^, rep from ^ to ^ once, rep from * to end.
Fasten off.

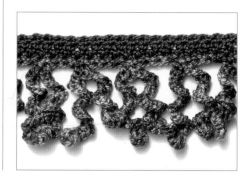

46 CORKSCREW FRINGE
Directory view, page 20

Skill level: Challenging/complex

 Cotton perle

METHOD

Make a foundation chain of the required length, or work row 1 directly into the item to be trimmed with right side facing.
(multiple of 3 stitches + 1)
Row 1: 1 ch, 1 dc in each ch to end, turn.
Row 2: As row 1.
Row 3: 1 ch, *3 dc, 9 ch, 4 dc in 2nd ch from hook, (4 dc in next st) 7 times, 1 sl st in last dc worked on fringe header, rep from * to end. Fasten off.

47 SUPER SEQUINS
Directory view, page 20

Skill level: Beginner/easy

 Cotton perle

 20 mm sequins in a range of colours

METHOD

Thread the sequins onto the yarn before starting work.
Make a foundation chain of the required length, or work row 1 directly into the item to be trimmed with right side facing.
(multiple of 6 stitches + 1)
Row 1: 1 ch, 1 dc in each ch to end, turn.
Row 2: 3 ch, *5 ch, bring down 1 sequin to be worked in next st, 1 dc in 2nd ch from hook, 1 dc in each of next 3 ch, 1 sl st in top of st on main section of fringe, 1 tr in each of next 5 dc, rep from * to end. Fasten off.

48 RINGLET FRINGE
Directory view, page 21

Skill level: Challenging/complex

 Cotton perle

METHOD

Make a foundation chain of the required length, or work row 1 directly into the item to be trimmed with right side facing.
(multiple of 3 stitches + 1)
Row 1: 1 ch, 1 dc in each ch to end, turn.
Row 2: 1 ch, *3 dc, 9 ch, 6 tr in 4th chain from hook, (6 tr in next st) 5 times, 1 sl st in last dc worked on fringe header, rep from * to end. Fasten off.

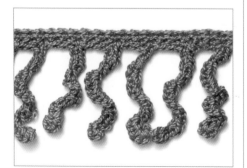

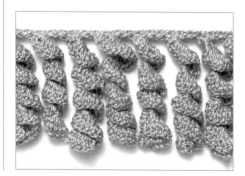

49 **SLIP FRINGE**
Directory view, page 21

Skill level: Beginner/easy

 Cotton perle

METHOD

Make a foundation chain of the required length, or work row 1 directly into the item to be trimmed with right side facing.
(multiple of 3 stitches + 1)
Row 1: 1 ch, 1 dc in each ch to end, turn.
Row 2: 3 ch, 1 tr in each st to end, turn.
Row 3: 1 ch, *2 dc, 9 ch, 1 sl st in 2nd ch from hook, 1 sl st in each of next 7 ch, 1 sl st in last dc worked on fringe header, 1 dc, rep from * to end. Fasten off.

 50 **TWISTED BULLIONS**
Directory view, page 21

Skill level: Challenging/complex

 Cotton perle

METHOD

Notes: Bullion stitch = yo 5 times, insert hook in next stitch and draw through a loop, yo and draw through all loops on hook, 1 chain.
Make a foundation chain of the required length, or work row 1 directly into the item to be trimmed with right side facing.
(multiple of 6 stitches + 1)
Row 1: 1 ch, 1 dc in each ch to end, turn.
Row 2: As row 1.
Row 3: As row 1.
Row 4: As row 1.
Row 5: 1 ch, *5 dc, 5 ch, 4 bullion sts in 2nd ch from hook, 3 sl st in fringe chain, 1 sl st in last dc worked on fringe header, 1 dc, rep from * to last st, 1 dc. Fasten off.

 51 **ONLY BEADS**
Directory view, page 21

Skill level: Intermediate

 Cotton perle

 3 mm glass seed beads

METHOD

Thread the beads onto the yarn before starting work, allowing 12 beads per loop. Make a foundation chain of the required length, or work row 1 directly into the item to be trimmed with right side facing.
(multiple of 3 stitches + 1)
Row 1: 1 ch, 1 dc in each ch to end, turn.
Row 2: As row 1.
Row 3: As row 1.
Row 4: 1 ch, *2 dc, bring down 12 beads and dc in next st (loop formed), rep from * to end. Fasten off.

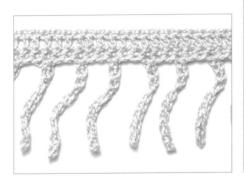

52 LATTICE FRINGE
Directory view, page 22

Skill level: Beginner/easy

 Cotton perle

METHOD

Make a foundation chain of the required length, or work row 1 directly into the item to be trimmed with right side facing.
(multiple of 6 stitches + 3)
Row 1: 1 ch, 1 dc in each ch to end, turn.
Row 2: 3 ch, 2 tr, *3 ch, miss 3 sts, 3 tr, rep from * to end, turn.
Row 3: As row 1. Fasten off.
Fringe: Using a single length of yarn, make two knots around row 3 in each 3-ch space.

53 PARTLY BEADS
Directory view, page 22

Skill level: Beginner/easy

 Cotton perle

 3 mm glass seed beads

METHOD

Make a foundation chain of the required length, or work row 1 directly into the item to be trimmed with right side facing.
(multiple of 3 stitches + 1)
Thread the beads onto the yarn before starting work, allowing 8 beads per loop.
Row 1: 1 ch, 1 dc in each ch to end, turn.
Row 2: As row 1.
Row 3: As row 1.
Row 4: 1 ch, *2 dc, bring down 8 beads, dc in next st, rep from * to end, turn.
Row 5: As row 1. Fasten off.

54 UNDULATING FRINGE
Directory view, page 22

Skill level: Challenging/complex

 Cotton perle

METHOD

Make a foundation chain of the required length, or work row 1 directly into the item to be trimmed with right side facing.
(multiple of 3 stitches + 1)
Row 1: 1 ch, 1 dc in each ch to end, turn.
Row 2: As row 1.
Row 3: 1 ch, *2 dc, 11 ch, 1 dc in 2nd ch from hook, 1 htr, 1 tr, 1 htr, 2 dc, 1 htr, 1 dc, 1 sl st in last dc worked on fringe header, 1 dc, rep from * to last st, 1 dc. Fasten off.

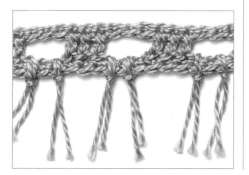

55 EYELASH FRINGE

Directory view, page 22

Skill level: Beginner/easy

 Worked in two yarns: cotton perle and eyelash yarn

METHOD

Make a foundation chain of the required length, or work row 1 directly into the item to be trimmed with right side facing. (any number of stitches)
Row 1: 1 ch, 1 dc in each ch to end, turn.
Row 2: 3 ch, 1 tr in each st to end, turn.
Row 3: As row 1. Fasten off.
Fringe: Knot one length of eyelash yarn around stem of each dc on row 3.

56 POPCORN FRINGE

Directory view, page 23

Skill level: Intermediate

 Double knitting (DK weight)

METHOD

Notes: Popcorn = work 5 tr in same st, slip last loop off hook, insert hook in top loop of first double treble, reinsert in top loop of last tr, pull this loop through to close the top of popcorn st.
Make a foundation chain of the required length, or work row 1 directly into the item to be trimmed with right side facing. (multiple of 5 stitches + 4)
Row 1: 1 ch, 1 dc in each ch to end, turn.
Row 2: 1 ch, 3 dc in front loop only, *popcorn, 4 dc in front loop only, rep from * to end, turn.
Row 3: 1 ch, 1 dc in front loop of each st to end, turn.
Row 4: As row 1. Fasten off.
Fringe: Knot three lengths of yarn into row 4, in line with the popcorn.

57 BEADED TRIANGLES

Directory view, page 23

Skill level: Intermediate

 Cotton perle

 5 mm glass seed beads

METHOD

Thread the beads onto the yarn before starting work.
Make a foundation chain of the required length, or work row 1 directly into the item to be trimmed with right side facing. (multiple of 8 stitches + 1)
Row 1: 1 ch, 1 dc in each ch to end, turn.
Row 2: 3 ch, 1 tr, *bring down a bead, 2 tr, rep from * to end, omitting bead on last rep, turn.
Row 3: As row 2.
Row 4: 1 ch, 1 dc in each st, turn.
Row 5: 1 ch, 1 dc in first st *6 ch, bring down and enclose a bead in 1 dc in 2nd ch from hook, 1 htr, 1 tr, 1 dtr, 1 trtr, miss 5 dc, 1 dc in each of next 3 dc, rep from * to end. Fasten off.
Fringe: Make a basic fringe (see page 119) using two lengths of yarn, placing them at the point with the bead.

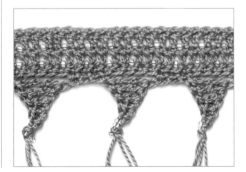

58 BEADED LOOPS

Directory view, page 23

Skill level: Intermediate

 Cotton perle

 3 mm glass seed beads

METHOD

Make a foundation chain of the required length, or work row 1 directly into the item to be trimmed with right side facing. (multiple of 4 stitches + 1)

Row 1: 1 ch, 1 dc in each ch to end, turn.
Row 2: 2 ch, *bring down a bead, 2 tr, rep from * to end, omitting bead on last rep, turn.
Row 3: As row 2.
Row 4: 1 ch, *3 dc, bring down 10 beads, 1 dc in next st to complete the fringe loop, rep from * to end. Fasten off.

59 CHEVRON FRINGE

Directory view, page 24

Skill level: Challenging/complex

 Cotton perle

METHOD

Make a foundation chain of the required length, or work row 1 directly into the item to be trimmed with right side facing. (multiple of 16 stitches + 2)

Row 1: 2 dc in 2nd ch from hook, *1 dc in each of next 7 ch, miss 1 ch, 1 dc in each of next 7 ch, 3 dc in next ch, rep from * to end, omitting 1 dc at end of last rep, turn.
Row 2: 1 ch, 1 dc in first dc, *1 dc in each of next 7 dc, miss 2 dc, 1 dc in next 7 dc, 3 dc into next dc, rep from * to end omitting 1 dc at end of last rep.
Rows 3–5: As row 2. Fasten off.
Fringe: Using the same colour of yarn, with right side and cast-off edge closest. The idea of this fringe is that there are two levels of fringe facing downwards towards row 5. Using the basic fringe method (see page 119), attach 3 yarn lengths to the lower level or cast-off edge. Upper level is worked on the second row from cast-on or fabric edge, allowing space to attach to an item.

60 BEADED CHEVRONS FRINGE

Directory view, page 24

Skill level: Intermediate

 Worked in fingering weight wool mixture yarn and cotton perle

 3 mm glass seed beads

METHOD

Make a foundation chain of the required length, or work row 1 directly into the item to be trimmed with right side facing. (multiple of 16 stitches + 2)

Row 1: 2 dc in 2nd ch from hook, *1 dc in each of next 7 ch, miss 1 ch, 1 dc in each of next 7 ch, 3 dc into next ch, rep from * to end, omitting 1 dc at end of last rep, turn.
Row 2: 1 ch, 1 dc into first dc, *1 dc into each of next 7 dc, miss 2 dc, 1 dc into next 7 dc, 3 dc into next dc, rep from * to end omitting 1 dc at end of last rep.
Rows 3–4: As row 2. Fasten off.
Fringe: Using the basic fringe method (see page 119), thread 2 beads onto 2 lengths of contrasting colour yarn. Keeping the beads in the centre, attach to the points of the chevrons.

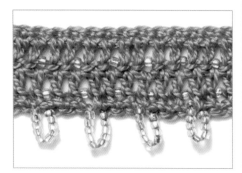

PEARL LEAF FRINGE
Directory view, page 25

Skill level: Challenging/complex

 Cotton perle

 10 mm pearl leaf beads

METHOD

Notes: Thread the beads onto the yarn before starting work.
Make a foundation chain of the required length, or work row 1 directly into the item to be trimmed with right side facing.
(multiple of 5 stitches + 2)
Row 1: 1 ch, 1 dc in each ch to end, turn.
Row 2: 2 ch, 1 htr, *bring down 2 beads, 5 htr, rep from * to end, turn.
Row 3: 1 ch, 1 tr in each htr to end.
Fasten off.

 DOUBLE MESH FRINGE
Directory view, page 25

Skill level: Beginner/easy

 Cotton perle

METHOD

Make a foundation chain of the required length, or work row 1 directly into the item to be trimmed with right side facing.
(multiple of 4 stitches + 1)
Row 1: 1 dc in 2nd ch from hook, 1 dc in each ch to end, turn.
Row 2: 1 ch, 1 dc in same st, 3 ch, miss 3 dc, 1 dc in next dc, turn.
Rows 3–4: As row 2. Fasten off.
Fringe: Insert 2 pairs of strands of prepared fringe yarn into each 3-ch sp on the final row.

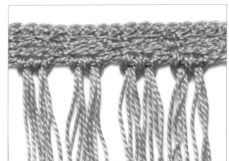

 GRANNY FRINGE
Directory view, page 25

Skill level: Beginner/easy

 Cotton perle

METHOD

Make a foundation chain of the required length, or work row 1 directly into the item to be trimmed with right side facing.
(multiple of 7 stitches + 1)
Row 1: 1 dc in 2nd ch from hook, 1 dc in each ch to end, turn.
Row 2: 3 ch, *2 tr, 1 ch, miss 1 dc, 1 tr in next dc, 2 ch, miss 2 dc, 1 tr in next dc, rep from * to end, turn.
Row 3: 3 ch, *2 ch, 1 tr in next tr, 1 ch, 1 tr in each of next 3 tr, rep from * to end, turn.
Fringe: Insert 2 strands of the prepared fringe yarn into each ch sp on the final row to end.

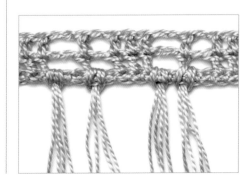

BRAIDS

SEE ALSO

Standard crochet abbreviations,
page 125
Refresher course, pages 110–125

 64 LIGHT AND DARK
Directory view, page 26

Skill level: Beginner/easy

 Worked in cotton perle in two colours: A and B

METHOD

Using yarn A make a foundation chain of the
required length, or work row 1 directly into
the item to be trimmed with right side facing.
(odd number of stitches)
Row 1: (A) 1 ch, 1 dc in each st or position
to end, turn.
Row 2: (A and B together) 1 ch, *miss 1 st,
2 tr in next st, rep from * to end. Fasten off
yarn A only.
Row 3: (B only) As row 1. Fasten off.

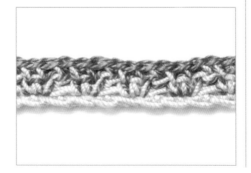

 65 SHINY SHELLS
Directory view, page 26

Skill level: Beginner/easy

 Cotton perle

 10 mm shell-shaped sequins in a range of colours

METHOD

Thread the sequins onto the yarn before
beginning.
Make a foundation chain of the required
length, or work row 1 directly into the item to
be trimmed with right side facing.
(multiple of 4 stitches + 1)
Row 1: 1 ch, 1 dc in each st or position to
end, turn.
Row 2: 1 ch, *bring down sequin in next dc,
3 dc, rep from * to end, turn.
Row 3: As row 1. Fasten off.

66 FANS AND COLUMNS
Directory view, page 26

Skill level: Beginner/easy

 Cotton perle

METHOD

Make a foundation chain of the required length, or work row 1 directly into the item to be trimmed with right side facing. (multiple of 10 stitches + 5)
Row 1: 1 ch, 1 dc in each st or position to end, turn.
Row 2: 3 ch, 4 tr, *miss 2 sts, 5 tr in next st, 2 ch, miss 2 sts, 5 tr, rep from * to end. Fasten off.

---

 67 FANS BRAID
Directory view, page 26

Skill level: Beginner/easy

 Cotton perle

METHOD

Make a foundation chain of the required length, or work row 1 directly into the item to be trimmed with right side facing. (multiple of 3 stitches + 1)
Row 1: 1 ch, 1 dc in each st or position to end, turn.
Row 2: 1 ch, *2 ch, miss 2 sts, 1 dc, rep from * to end, turn.
Row 3: 3 ch, 3 tr in each 2-ch sp to end. Fasten off.

---

 68 SOFT CENTRE
Directory view, page 27

Skill level: Beginner/easy

 Worked in two yarns: cotton perle (smooth) and mohair (fluffy)

METHOD

Using the smooth yarn, make a foundation chain of the required length, or work row 1 directly into the item to be trimmed with right side facing. (odd number of stitches)
Row 1: (smooth yarn) 1 ch, 1 dc in each st or position to end. Fasten off, turn.
Row 2: (fluffy yarn) 3 ch, *2 tr in next st, 1 tr, rep from * to end, turn.
Row 3: (fluffy yarn) As row 1. Fasten off, turn.
Row 4: (smooth yarn) As row 1. Fasten off.

---

 69 BLOCKS BRAID
Directory view, page 27

Skill level: Beginner/easy

 Worked in cotton perle in two colours: A and B

METHOD

Using yarn A, make a foundation chain of the required length, or work row 1 directly into the item to be trimmed with right side facing. (multiple of 3 stitches + 1)
Row 1: (A) 2 ch, 1 htr in each st or position to end. Fasten off, turn.
Row 2: (B) 2 ch, *2 htr into next st, 1 ch, miss 1 st, 1 htr in next st, rep from * to end. Fasten off, turn.
Row 3: (A) 1 ch, 1 dc in each st to end. Fasten off.

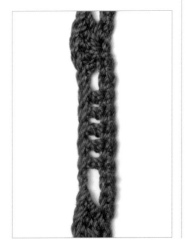

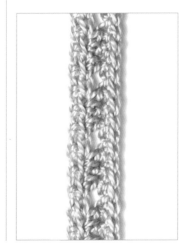

70 MOVING BLOCKS
Directory view, page 27

Skill level: Intermediate

 Cotton perle

METHOD

Make a foundation chain of the required length, or work row 1 directly into the item to be trimmed with right side facing. (multiple of 8 stitches + 1)
Row 1: 5 ch, 1 tr in 9th ch from hook, 5 tr, *2 ch, miss 2 sts, 6 tr, rep from * to end, turn.
Row 2: As row 1. Fasten off.

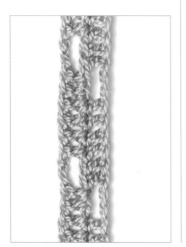

71 FINE BLOCKS
Directory view, page 27

Skill level: Intermediate

 Cotton perle

METHOD

Make a foundation chain of the required length, or work row 1 directly into the item to be trimmed with right side facing. (multiple of 13 stitches + 3)
Row 1: 4 ch, 1 tr in 7th ch from hook, 5 tr, (1 ch, miss 1 st, 1 tr) 3 times, 1 ch, *miss 1 st, 6 tr, (1 ch, miss 1 st, 1 tr) 3 times, 1 ch, rep from * to last st, 1 tr, turn.
Row 2: 4 ch, *(miss 1 st, 1 tr, 1 ch in next st) 3 times, 1 ch, 6 tr, rep from * to last 2 sts, 1 ch, miss 1 st, 1 tr in last st. Fasten off.

72 LAZY FANS
Directory view, page 27

Skill level: Intermediate

 Cotton perle

METHOD

Make a foundation chain of the required length, or work row 1 directly into the item to be trimmed with right side facing. (multiple of 7 stitches + 1)
Row 1: 1 ch, *2 dc, miss 1 st, 4 tr in next st, miss 1 st, 2 dc, rep from * to end. Fasten off.

73 WAVES BRAID
Directory view, page 27

Skill level: Intermediate

 Cotton perle

METHOD

Make a foundation chain of the required length, or work row 1 directly into the item to be trimmed with right side facing. (multiple of 12 stitches)
Row 1: 3 ch, 1 tr in same st, *3 tr, tr2tog twice, 3 tr, 2 tr in next st twice, rep from * to end. The last rep will end with only one 2 tr in next st. Fasten off.

74 BOBBLES BRAID
Directory view, page 28

Skill level: Intermediate

 Cotton perle

METHOD

Notes: bobble = tr4tog in next st.
Make a foundation chain of the required length, or work row 1 directly into the item to be trimmed with right side facing. (multiple of 7 stitches + 1)
Row 1: 1 ch, 1 dc in each st or position to end, turn.
Row 2: 3 ch, *2 tr, miss 1 st, bobble, miss 1 st, 2 tr, rep from * to end, turn.
Row 3: As row 1. Fasten off.

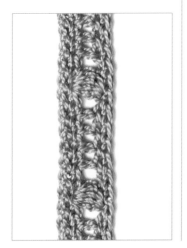

75 RANDOM BOBBLES
Directory view, page 28

Skill level: Intermediate

 Cotton perle

METHOD

Notes: bobble = tr4tog in next st.
Make a foundation chain of the required length, or work row 1 directly into the item to be trimmed with right side facing. (multiple of 6 stitches + 3)
Row 1: 1 ch, 1 dc in each st or position to end, turn.
Row 2: 1 ch, *2 dc, bobble, 3 dc, rep from * to end, turn.
Row 3: As row 1.
Row 4: As row 2, but place bobbles at random. Fasten off.

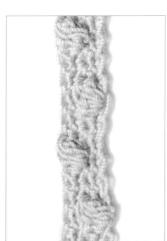

76 JAZZY BRAID
Directory view, page 28

Skill level: Beginner/easy

 Cotton perle

 5 mm glass seed beads

METHOD

Thread the beads onto the yarn before beginning.
Make a foundation chain of the required length, or work row 1 directly into the item to be trimmed with right side facing. (multiple of 3 stitches + 1)
Row 1: 1 ch, *bring down a bead to work into next dc, 2 dc, rep from * to end. Fasten off.

77 RIDGE BRAID
Directory view, page 28

Skill level: Intermediate

 Cotton perle

METHOD

Notes: bobble = tr4tog in next st.
Make a foundation chain of the required length, or work row 1 directly into the item to be trimmed with right side facing. (multiple of 6 stitches + 1)
Row 1: 1 ch, 1 dc in each st or position to end, turn.
Row 2: 1 ch, *bobble, 5 dc, rep from * to end, turn.
Row 3: As row 1. Fasten off.

78 STRIPED BRAID
Directory view, page 28

Skill level: Intermediate

Worked in cotton perle in three colours: A, B and C

METHOD

Using colour A, make a foundation chain of the required length, or work row 1 directly into the item to be trimmed with right side facing. (any number of stitches)
Row 1: (A) 1 ch, 1 dc in each st or position to end. Fasten off, turn.
Row 2: (B) As row 1.
Row 3: (C) As row 1.
Row 4: (A) As row 1.

79 SPRAY BRAID
Directory view, page 28

Skill level: Beginner/easy

Worked in cotton perle in two colours: A and B

METHOD

Using colour A make a foundation chain of the required length, or work row 1 directly into the item to be trimmed with right side facing. (any number of stitches)
Row 1: (A) 1 ch, 1 dc in each st or position to end, turn.
Row 2: (A) 2 ch, 1 htr in each st to end. Fasten off, turn.
Row 3: (B) 1 ch, *1 tr into dc on row 1, 1 dc, rep from * to last st, 1 tr, turn.
Row 4: (B) As row 1. Fasten off, turn.
Row 5: (A) As row 3, working tr into tr on row 3.
Row 6: (A) As row 1. Fasten off.

80 EYELET BRAID
Directory view, page 29

Skill level: Intermediate

Cotton perle

METHOD

Make a foundation chain of the required length, or work row 1 directly into the item to be trimmed with right side facing. (multiple of 8 stitches + 1)
Row 1: 1 ch, 1 dc in each st or position to end, turn.
Row 2: 3 ch, *(1 ch, miss 1 st, 1 tr in next st) 3 times, 2 tr, rep from * to end, turn.
Row 3: As row 1. Fasten off.

81 LAYER BRAID
Directory view, page 29

Skill level: Intermediate

Worked in cotton perle in two colours: A and B

METHOD

Using colour A, make a foundation chain of the required length, or work row 1 directly into the item to be trimmed with right side facing. (odd number of stitches)
Row 1: (A) 1 ch, 1 dc in each st or position to end. Fasten off, turn.
Row 2: (B) 3 ch, *1 tr in each st to end, turn.
Row 3: (B) As row 1. Fasten off, turn.
Row 4: (A) 1 ch, *1 dc, 1 tr in next st on row 2, rep from * to end. Fasten off.

82 BOBBLE STEPS
Directory view, page 29

Skill level: Intermediate

 Worked in cotton perle in two colours: A and B

METHOD

Notes: bobble = tr4tog in next st.

Using colour A, make a foundation chain of the required length, or work row 1 directly into the item to be trimmed with right side facing. (multiple of 8 stitches + 1)

Row 1: (A) 1 ch, 1 dc in each st or position to end. Fasten off, turn.

Row 2: (B) 1 ch, *bobble, 7 dc, rep from * to end, turn.

Row 3: (B) As row 1. Do not fasten off.

Row 4: (B) 1 ch, *3 dc, bobble, 4 dc, rep from * to end, turn.

Row 5: (B) As row 1. Do not fasten off.

Row 6: (B) 1 ch, *6 dc, bobble, 1 dc, rep from * to end, turn.

Row 7: (B) As row 1.

Row 8: (A) As row 1. Fasten off.

83 PYRAMIDS BRAID
Directory view, page 29

Skill level: Intermediate

 Cotton perle

METHOD

Make a foundation chain of the required length, or work row 1 directly into the item to be trimmed with right side facing. (multiple of 6 + 1 stitches)

Row 1: 1 ch, 1 dc in each st or position to end, turn.

Row 2: 1 ch, 1 dc in first st *6 ch, 1 dc in 2nd ch from hook, 1 dc in next ch, 1 htr in next ch, 1 tr in next ch, 1 dtr in next ch, 1 trtr in last of the 6 ch, miss 5 ch on row 1, 1 dc in next dc, rep from * to end. Fasten off.

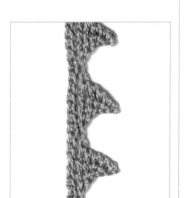

84 SHEATHS BRAID
Directory view, page 29

Skill level: Intermediate

 Cotton perle

METHOD

Make a foundation chain of the required length, or work row 1 directly into the item to be trimmed with right side facing. (multiple of 7 + 4 chains)

Row 1: Working along one side of the foundation chain only, 1 dc in 2nd ch from hook, 1 dc in each of next 2 ch, *3 ch, miss 3 ch, 1 dc in each of next 4 ch, rep from * to end.

Row 2: Working along the other side of the foundation chain, 3 ch, *3 ch, 5 tr in next 3-ch loop, rep from * to last 3 dc, 1 ch, 1 tr in last st. Fasten off.

85 LONG WAVES
Directory view, page 30

Skill level: Intermediate

 Cotton perle

METHOD

Make a foundation chain of the required length, or work row 1 directly into the item to be trimmed with right side facing. (multiple of 12 stitches)

Row 1: 1 ch, *1 dc, 2 htr, 2 tr, 2 dtr, 2 tr, 2 htr, 1 dc, rep from * to end, turn.

Row 2: 1 ch, 1 dc in each st to end, turn.

Row 3: 4 ch, *2 tr, 2 htr, 2 dc, 2 htr, 2 tr, 1 dtr, rep from * to end. Fasten off.

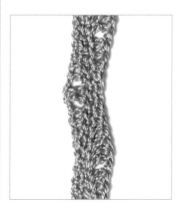

86 ANGLED CHEVRONS
Directory view, page 30

Skill level: Intermediate

 Cotton perle

 2 mm glass seed beads

METHOD

Thread the beads onto the yarn before starting work.
Make a foundation chain of the required length, or work row 1 directly into the item to be trimmed with right side facing.
(multiple of 14 stitches + 1)
Row 1: 1 ch, 2 dc in 2nd ch from hook, *1 dc in each of next 8 ch, miss 1 ch, 1 dc in each of next 4 ch, 3 tr into next ch, rep from * to end, omitting 1 dc at end of last rep, turn.
Row 2: 1 ch, 2 dc in first dc, *1 dc into each of next 3 dc, bring down 1 bead to work into next dc, miss 1 dc, bring down 1 bead to work into next dc, 1 dc in each of next 8 dc, 3 dc into next ch, rep from * to last long section of chevron, end with 2 dc in last st. Fasten off.

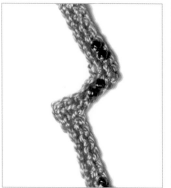

87 SHALLOW FILET BRAID
Directory view, page 30

Skill level: Intermediate

 Cotton perle

METHOD

Make a foundation chain of the required length, or work row 1 directly into the item to be trimmed with right side facing.
(multiple of 5 stitches + 1)
Row 1: 1 ch, 1 dc in each st or position to end, turn.
Row 2: As row 1.
Row 3: 3 ch, *4 ch, miss 4 ch, 1 tr in next dc, rep from * to end.
Row 4: As row 1.
Row 5: As row 1. Fasten off.

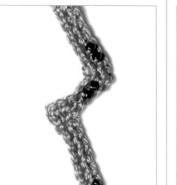

89 DEEP FILET BRAID
Directory view, page 30

Skill level: Intermediate

 Cotton perle

METHOD

Make a foundation chain of the required length, or work row 1 directly into the item to be trimmed with right side facing.
(multiple of 6 stitches + 1)
Row 1: 1 ch, 1 dc in each st or position to end, turn.
Rows 2 & 3: As row 1.
Row 4: 1 ch, 1 dc in first st, *3 ch, miss 2 dc, 1 dc in next dc, rep from * to end, turn.
Row 5: *2 ch, 1 dc in next 3-ch loop, rep from * to last st, 1 dc, turn.
Row 6: 1 ch, 1 dc in each st to end, turn.
Row 7: As row 6. Fasten off.

90 LUXURIOUS BRAID
Directory view, page 30

Skill level: Challenging/complex

 Cotton perle

METHOD

Make a foundation chain of the required length, or work row 1 directly into the item to be trimmed with right side facing.
(multiple of 3 stitches + 1)
Row 1: 1 ch, 1 dc in each st or position to end, turn.
Row 2: As row 1.
Row 3: 1 ch, *3 dc, 4 ch, rep from * to end omitting 4 ch on last rep, turn.
Row 4: 1 ch, *3 dc, 8 tr in 4-ch loop, *rep from * to last 3 sts, 3 dc. Fasten off.
Return to the beginning of foundation row, rep rows 1–4. Fasten off.

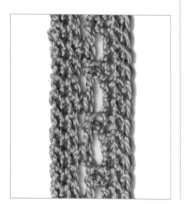
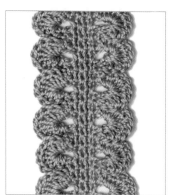

MOTIFS

SEE ALSO

Standard crochet abbreviations,
page 125
Refresher course,
pages 110–125

90 SUN DAISY

Directory view, page 31

Skill level: Beginner/easy

 Cotton perle

METHOD

Notes: tr2tog = work I tr into each of next 2 tr until I loop of each remains on hook, yo and through all 3 loops on hook.
Make 6 ch, sl st into first ch to form a ring.
Round 1: I ch, 15 dc in ring, sl st into first dc.
Round 2: (3 ch, tr2tog, 3 ch, sl st into next tr) 5 times, placing last sl st into last tr of previous round. Fasten off.

91 GOLDEN PANSY

Directory view, page 31

Skill level: Beginner/easy

 Cotton perle

METHOD

Notes: dtr2tog in next st = work 2 dtr in next st until I loop of each remains on hook, yo and through all 4 loops on hook.
Make 5 ch, sl st into first ch to form a ring.
Round 1: I ch, 12 dc into ring, sl st into first dc.
Round 2: 4 ch, dtr2tog in next st, 4 ch, sl st into each of next 2 tr, rep from * 3 times, omitting I sl st at end of last rep.
Make stalk: 7 ch, I dc into 2nd ch from hook, I dc into each of next 5 ch. Fasten off.

92 SUNBURST
Directory view, page 31

Skill level: Beginner/easy

 Cotton perle

METHOD

Make 6 ch, sl st into first ch to form a ring.
Round 1: 1 ch, (1 dc, 12 ch) 12 times into ring, sl st into first dc. Fasten off.

93 CLOVER
Directory view, page 31

Skill level: Beginner/easy

 Cotton perle

METHOD

Notes: dtr3tog = work 1 dtr into each of same place as last st and the next 2 dc until 1 loop of each remains on hook, yo and through all 4 loops on hook.
Make 5 ch, sl st into first ch to form a ring.
Round 1: 1 ch, 10 dc into ring, sl st into first dc.
Round 2: 1 ch, 1 dc into first tr, *4 ch, dtr3tog, 4 ch, 1 dc in same place as last st, 1 dc in next dc, rep from * twice.
Make stalk: 7 ch (or number required), turn, 1 dc in 2nd ch from hook, 1 dc in each ch, sl st in first dc on round. Fasten off.

94 IRISH SHAMROCK
Directory view, page 31

Skill level: Intermediate

 Cotton perle

METHOD

Make 6 ch, sl st into first ch to form a ring.
Round 1: 1 ch, 18 dc into ring, sl st into first dc.
Round 2: 8 ch, miss 4 dc, sl st in next dc, 10 ch, miss 4 dc, sl st into next dc, 8 ch, sl st in next 2 dc.
Make stalk: 12 ch, 1 dc in 3rd ch from hook, 1 dc into each of next 9 ch, sl st into last dc.
Round 3: 16 dc in next 8-ch loop, 20 dc in next 10-ch loop, 16 dc in next 8-ch loop, sl st to beg of stalk. Fasten off.

LINKED PETALS
Directory view, page 32

Skill level: Beginner/easy

 Cotton perle

METHOD

Notes: Bobble: tr4tog in next st = 4 tr into next dc until 1 loop of each remains on hook, yo and through all 5 loops.
Make 6 ch, sl st in to first ch to form a ring.
Round 1: 1 ch, 14 dc in ring, sl st into first dc.
Round 2: 3 ch, bobble in next dc, 5 ch, *miss 1 dc, 1 bobble in next tr, 5 ch, rep from * to end, sl st in top of first bobble. Fasten off.

 SUNSHINE
Directory view, page 32

Skill level: Intermediate

 Cotton perle

METHOD

Make 9 ch, sl st in first ch to form a ring.
Round 1: 1 ch, 18 dc in ring, sl st into first dc.
Round 2: *9 ch, 1 dc in 4th ch from hook, 1 htr in each of next 2 ch, 1 tr in each of next 3 ch, miss 2 dc on ring, sl st in next dc, rep from * to end, placing last st into same st as sl st of previous round. Fasten off.

 ENGLISH ROSE
Directory view, page 32

Skill level: Intermediate

 Cotton perle

METHOD

Make 8 ch, sl st into first ch to form a ring.
Round 1: 3 ch, 1 tr in ring, (6 ch, 3 tr in ring) 5 times, 6 ch, 1 tr in ring, sl st in top of ch at beg of round.
Round 2: 1 ch, *(1 dc, 1 htr, 7 tr, 1 htr, 1 dc), in next 6-ch loop, 1 ch, miss 1 tr, 1 sl st in next tr, rep from * 5 times, working last sl st in 3rd of 3 ch at beg of previous round. Fasten off.

IRISH LEAF
Directory view, page 32

Skill level: Beginner/easy

 Cotton perle

METHOD

Notes: Work into back loop only on each repeat of row 2.
Make 11 ch.
Row 1: Working into one loop only along first side of ch, 1 dc into 2nd ch from hook, 1 dc in each of next 8 ch, 3 dc in last ch, working in one loop only along other side of foundation ch, 1 dc in each of next 7 ch, turn.
Row 2: Working in back loop only, 1 ch, 1 dc in first dc, 1 dc in each of next 7 dc, 3 dc in next dc, 1 dc in each of next 7 dc, turn.
Rep row 2 as many times as desired.
Fasten off.

 **PRINCELY PETALS**
Directory view, page 32

Skill level: Intermediate

Cotton perle

METHOD

Round 1: 10 ch, sl st into first ch, (9 ch, sl st in same ch as last sl st) twice.
Round 2: *1 ch, (2 dc, 1 htr, 11 tr, 1 htr, 2 dc), in next 9-ch loop, 1 ch sl st into same sl st as first round, rep from * to end, sl st to first st. Fasten off.

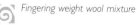 **FAN CIRCLE**
Directory view, page 33

Skill level: Beginner/easy

Fingering weight wool mixture

METHOD

Make 6 ch, sl st into first ch to form a ring.
Round 1: 6 ch, (3 dtr in ring, 2 ch) 5 times, 2 dtr in ring, sl st into 4th of 6 ch at beg of round.
Round 2: 1 ch, 1 dc in 2-ch loop, *6 ch, miss 3 dtr, 1 dc in next 2-ch loop, rep from * to end, omitting dc at end of last rep, sl st in dc at beg of round.
Round 3: 1 ch, (1 dc, 1 htr, 1 tr, 3 dtr, 1 tr, 1 htr, 1 dc) into each 6-ch loop, sl st in first dc. Fasten off.

SILHOUETTE CLOVER
Directory view, page 33

Skill level: Intermediate

 Cotton perle

METHOD

Round 1: 16 ch, sl st in first ch (first loop formed), (15 ch, sl st in same ch as last sl st) twice.
Round 2: 1 ch, (28 htr in next loop, 1 sl st in same ch as sl st of first round) 3 times.
Make stalk: 12 ch, 1 htr in 3rd ch from hook, 1 htr in each ch to end, sl st in same ch as last sl st. Fasten off.

 WESTERN MOTIF
Directory view, page 33

Skill level: Intermediate

 Cotton perle

METHOD

Make 8 ch, sl st into first ch to form a ring.
Round 1: 1 ch, 15 dc in ring, sl st in first ch.
Round 2: 12 ch, miss 1 dc, *1 dtr in next dc, 8 ch, rep from * to end, sl st in 4th of 12 ch.
Round 3: 1 ch, *(1 dc, 1 htr, 1 tr, 3 dtr, 3 ch, sl st in 3rd ch from hook, 2 dtr, 1 tr, 1 htr, 1 dc) in 8-ch loop, rep from * to end, sl st in first ch. Fasten off.

 LAYERED ROSE
Directory view, page 34

Skill level: Intermediate

 *Cotton perle*

METHOD

Make 8 ch, sl st in first ch to form a ring.
Round 1: 1 ch, 18 dc, sl st in first ch.
Round 2: 6 ch, miss first 2 dc, *1 htr in next dc, 4 ch, miss 2 tr, rep from * to end, sl st in 2nd of 6 ch at beg of round.
Round 3: 1 ch, (1 dc, 1 htr, 3 tr, 1 htr, 1 dc) in each 4-ch loop, sl st in first tr. (6 petals)
Round 4: sl st in back of the nearest htr of 2nd round, *5 ch, working behind each petal of previous round sl st in next htr of 2nd round, rep from * to end.
Round 5: 1 ch, (1 dc, 1 htr, 5 tr, 1 htr, 1 dc) in each 5-ch loop join with a sl st in first dc.
Round 6: sl st in back of sl st of 4th round, *6 ch, working behind each petal of previous round, sl st in next sl st of 4th round, rep from * to end.
Round 7: (1 dc, 1 htr, 6 tr, 1 htr, 1 dc) in each 6-ch loop, join with a sl st in first dc. Fasten off.

 **ELEGANT ROSE**
Directory view, page 34

Skill level: Challenging/complex

 Cotton perle

METHOD

Notes: Picot = make 3 ch, sl st into first of these ch.
Make 8 ch, sl st in first ch to form a ring.
Round 1: 3 ch, 15 tr in ring, sl st in 3rd of 3 ch at beg of round.
Round 2: 5 ch, (1 tr in next tr, 2 ch) 15 times, sl st in 3rd in of 5 ch at beg of round.
Round 3: 1 ch, 3 dc in each of the 16 2-ch loops, sl st in first dc.
Round 4: 1 ch, 1 dc in same dc as the last sl st, *6 ch, miss 5 dc, 1 dc in next dc, rep from * 6 times, 6 ch, sl st in first dc.
Round 5: sl st in first 6-ch loop, 1 ch, (1 dc, 1 htr, 6 tr, 1 htr, 1 dc) in each of the 8 6-ch loops, sl st in first dc, (8 petals worked).
Round 6: 1 ch, working behind each petal of previous round, 1 dc in first dc on 4th round, *7 ch, 1 dc in next dc on 4th round, rep from * 6 times, 7 ch, sl st in first dc.

Round 7: sl st in first 7-ch loop, 1 ch, (1 dc, 1 htr, 7 tr, 1 htr, 1 dc) in each of the 8 7-ch loops, sl st in first dc.
Round 8: 1 ch, working behind each petal of previous round, 1 dc in first dc on 6th round, *8 ch, 1 dc in next dc on 6th round, rep from * 6 times, 8 ch, sl st in first dc.
Round 9: sl st in first 8-ch loop, 1 ch, (1 dc, 1 htr, 3 tr, picot, 2 tr, picot, 3 tr, 1 htr, 1 dc) in each of the 8 8-ch loops, sl st in first tr. Fasten off.

 **FLOWER SILHOUETTE**
Directory view, page 34

Skill level: Intermediate

 Cotton perle

METHOD

Make 20 ch, sl st in first ch to form a ring.
Round 1: 1 ch, 38 dc in ring, sl st in first dc.
Round 2: *9 ch, miss 6 dc, 1 dc in next dc, rep from * 4 times, sl st in each of next 3 dc.
Round 3: 2 dc in each 9-ch loop, 1 dc in each of next 3 sl st, sl st to first dc.
Round 4: 3 ch, 1 tr in each dc, sl st in first dc of round.
Make stem: 14 ch, 1 dc in 3rd ch from hook, 1 dc in each of next 11 ch. Fasten off.

EASTERN MOTIF
Directory view, page 35

Skill level: Intermediate

 Cotton perle

METHOD

Make 8 ch, sl st in first ch to form a ring.
Round 1: 1 ch, 16 dc in ring, sl st in first dc.
Round 2: 4 ch, 2 dtr in first dc, 3 dtr in next dc, 5 ch, (miss 2 dc, 3 dtr in each of next 2 dc, 5 ch) 3 times, sl st in top of 4 ch at beg of round.
Round 3: 1 ch, *(1 htr, 1 tr) in next dtr, 2 dtr in each of next 2 dtr, (1 tr, 1 htr) in next dtr, 1 dc in next dtr, 1 dc in each of next 2 dc, 3 dc in next ch, 1 dc in each of next 2 ch, 1 dc in next dtr, rep from * 3 times, omit 1 dc at the end of last rep, sl st in first dc. Fasten off.

INTRICATE PETALS
Directory view, page 35

Skill level: Intermediate

 Cotton perle

METHOD

Make 12 ch, sl st in first ch to form a ring.
Round 1: 1 ch, 24 dc in ring, sl st in first dc.
Round 2: 12 ch, *miss next dc, 1 dc in next dc, turn, 3 ch, 1 tr in each of first 7 ch of 12-ch arch, turn, 3 ch, miss first tr, 1 tr in each of next 6 tr, 1 tr in top of 3 ch (first block made), miss next dc on ring, ** 1 dtr in next dc, 8 ch *, rep from * to * 4 times, and rep from * to ** once, sl st in 4th of 12 ch at beg of round. Fasten off.

ELEGANT PETALS
Directory view, page 35

Skill level: Challenging/complex

 Cotton perle

METHOD

Notes: Picot = make 3 ch, sl st in first of these ch.
Make 6 ch, sl st in first ch to form a ring.
Round 1: 1 ch, 15 dc in ring, sl st in first ch.
Round 2: 1 ch, *2 dc, (1 dc, 9 ch, 1 dc) in next tr, 1 dc, rep from * to end, sl st in first dc.
Round 3: 1 ch, *1 dc, miss 1 dc, 21 tr in 9-ch loop, miss 1 dc, rep from * to end, sl st in first dc.
Round 4: 1 ch, *1 dc in dc of round 2, 5 ch, miss 5 tr, 1 dc in next tr, picot, 5 ch in first dc, miss 4 tr, 1 dc in next tr (middle tr in loop), picot, 5 ch, rep from * to end, sl st in first dc. Fasten off.

109 SHELL FLOWER
Directory view, page 35

Skill level: Intermediate

 Cotton perle

METHOD

Make 6 ch, sl st in first ch to form a ring.
Round 1: 3 ch, 15 tr in ring, sl st in 3rd of 3 ch at beg of round.
Round 2: 1 ch, 1 dc in same st, 1 dc in next tr, *(1 dc, 7 ch, 1 dc) in next tr, 1 dc in each of next 3 tr, rep from * 3 times, omitting 3 dc at end of last rep, sl st in first ch.
Round 3: 1 ch, 1 dc in same st, *(2 htr, 17 tr, 2 htr), in 7-ch loop, miss 2 dc, 1 dc in next dc, rep from * 3 times, omitting 1 dc at end of last rep, sl st in first dc. Fasten off.

110 TRELLIS MOTIF
Directory view, page 36

Skill level: Intermediate

 Cotton perle

METHOD

Make 6 ch, sl st in first ch to form a ring.
Round 1: 3 ch, 15 tr in ring, sl st in 3rd of 3 ch at beg of round.
Round 2: 5 ch, 1 tr in same st, *1 ch, miss 1 tr, (1 tr, 2 ch, 1 tr), in next tr, rep from * 6 times, 1 ch, sl st in 3rd of 5 ch at beg of round.
Round 3: sl st in first 2-ch loop, 3 ch, (1 tr, 2 ch, 2 tr) in same loop, *1 ch, (2 tr, 2 ch, 2 tr), in next 2-ch loop, rep from * 6 times, 1 ch, sl st in 3rd of 3 ch at beg of round.
Round 4: sl st in next tr and first 2-ch loop, 3 ch, 6 tr in same loop, 1 dc in next 1-ch loop, (7 tr in next 2-ch loop, 1 dc in next 1-ch loop) 7 times, sl st in 3rd of 3 ch at beg of round. Fasten off.

111 MARIGOLD
Directory view, page 36

Skill level: Beginner/easy

 Cotton perle

METHOD

Notes: trtr3tog = 3 trtr in 2-ch loop until 1 loop of each remains on hook, yo and through all 4 loops on hook.
fpdc (front post dc) = work 1 dc around stem of next tr, inserting hook from right to left.
Make 4 ch, sl st in first ch to form a ring.
Round 1: 5 ch, (1 tr in ring, 2 ch) 5 times, sl st in 3rd of 5 ch at beg of round.
Round 2: 5 ch, *trtr3tog in 2-ch loop, 5 ch, 1 fpdc around stem of next tr, 4 ch, rep from * 5 times, sl st in first ch of this round. Fasten off.

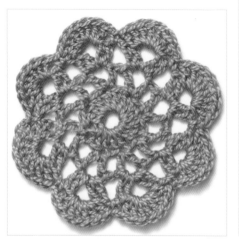

112 STAR FLOWER
Directory view, page 36

Skill level: Beginner/easy

 Cotton perle

METHOD

Make 4 ch, sl st in first ch to form a ring.
Round 1: 3 ch, 15 tr in ring, sl st in 3rd of
5 ch at beg of round.
Round 2: 4 ch, (miss 1 tr, 1 dc in next st,
3 ch) 7 times, sl st into first ch at beg of
round.
Round 3: 7 ch, (1 dc in next dc, 4 ch)
7 times, sl st in 3rd of 7 ch.
Round 4: 1 ch, *(1 dc, 1 htr, 1 tr, 1 htr,
1 dc) in each 4-ch loop, sl st in first ch.
Fasten off.

113 CIRCLED LACE
Directory view, page 36

Skill level: Intermediate

 Cotton perle

METHOD

Make 10 ch, sl st in first ch to form a ring.
Round 1: 3 ch, 23 tr in ring, sl st in 3rd of
5 ch at beg of round.
Round 2: 3 ch, (2 tr in next tr, 1 tr in each of
next 2 tr) to end, omitting final tr, sl st in 3rd
of 3 ch at beg of round.
Round 3: 3 ch, 1 tr in each of next 2 tr,
2 ch, 2 tr in next tr, *1 tr in each of next
3 tr, 2 ch, 2 tr in next tr, rep from * to end,
sl st in 3rd of 3 ch at beg of round.
Round 4: 3 ch, 1 tr in each of next 2 tr,
*2 ch, 1 tr in next 2-ch loop, 2 ch, 1 tr in
each of next 5 tr, rep from * to end, omitting
final 3 tr, sl st in 3rd of 3 ch at beg of round.
Round 5: 3 ch, 1 tr in next tr, *5 ch, miss
1 tr, 1 tr in next tr, 5 ch, miss 1 tr, 1 tr in each
of next 3 tr, rep from * to end, omitting 2 tr
at end of last rep, sl st into 3rd of 3 ch at beg
of round. Fasten off.

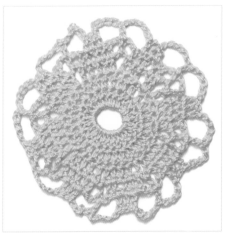

114 FRAMED FLOWER
Directory view, page 37

Skill level: Intermediate

 Cotton perle

METHOD

Make 12 ch, sl st in first ch to form a ring.
Round 1: 1 ch, 24 dc in ring, sl st in first dc.
Round 2: 12 ch, miss next dc, 1 dc in next
dc, turn, 3 ch, 1 tr in each of first 7 ch, turn,
3 ch, 1 tr in each of next 6 tr, 1 tr in top of
3 ch, (first block made), *miss next dc in ring,
1 dtr in next dc, 8 ch, miss next dc, 1 dc in
next dc, turn, 3 ch, 1 tr in each of first 7 ch,
turn, 3 ch, 1 tr in each of next 6 tr, 1 tr in top
of 3 ch for next block. Rep from * 4 times,
sl st in fourth of 12 ch at beg of round.
Round 3: sl st to top of 3 ch at corner of
first block, 1 ch, 1 dc into top of 3 ch, 13 ch,
*1 dc in 3rd of 3 ch at top of next block,
13 ch, rep from * to end, sl st in first dc.
Round 4: 1 ch, 1 dc in each st to end.
Fasten off.

SQUARE FRAMED CIRCLES
Directory view, page 37

Skill level: Intermediate

Cotton perle

METHOD

Make 6 ch, sl st in first ch to form a ring.
Round 1: 3 ch, 15 tr in ring, sl st in 3rd of 3 ch at beg of round.
Round 2: 1 ch, 1 dc into same st, 1 dc in next tr, *(1 dc, 7 ch, 1 dc) in next tr, 1 dc in each of next 3 tr, rep from * 3 times, omitting 2 dc at end of last rep, sl st in first dc.
Round 3: 1 ch, 1 dc in same st, *(2 htr, 17 tr, 2 htr) in next 7-ch loop, miss 2 dc, 1 dc in next dc, rep from * 3 times, omitting 1 dc at end of last rep, sl st in first tr.
Round 4: sl st in each of next 2 htr and 6 tr, 1 ch, 1 dc in same st, 9 ch, miss 5 tr, 1 dc in next tr, *7 ch, 1 dc in sixth tr of next loop, 9 ch, miss 5 tr, 1 dc in next tr, rep from * to end, 7 ch, sl st in first dc.
Round 5: 3 ch, *(8 tr, 1 dtr, 8 tr) in 9-ch loop, 1 tr in next dc, 7 tr in next 7-ch loop, 1 tr in next dc, rep from * 3 times, omitting 1 tr at end of last rep, sl st in 3rd ch at beg of round. Fasten off.

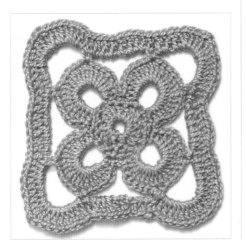

 ## PINWHEEL
Directory view, page 37

Skill level: Beginner/easy

Cotton perle

METHOD

Make 6 ch, sl st in first ch to form a ring.
Round 1: 3 ch, 2 tr in ring, (2 ch, 3 tr in ring) 5 times, 2 ch, sl st in top of 3 ch.
Round 2: sl st in next 2 tr and 2-ch loop, 4 ch, (2 dtr, 2 ch, 3 dtr) in 2-ch loop, (3 dtr, 2 ch, 3 dtr) in each 2-ch loop to end, sl st in top of 4 ch. Fasten off.

  ## CHRYSANTHEMUM
Directory view, page 38

Skill level: Beginner/easy

Cotton perle  *1 brooch back for fastening*

METHOD

Make 21 ch, 1 sl st in 2nd ch from hook, 1 sl st in each ch to end, turn, *miss first st, sl st in each of next 2 sts, 17 ch, miss first ch, sl st in each ch to end, turn *, rep from * to * until approximately 60 to 70 petals have been completed. Fasten off.
To make up: Beginning at one end of the work, fold the base of the petals round and round and secure with sewing stitches, forming a slight spiral at the very beginning. Continue until all of the petals have been secured.
Attach to the brooch backing if required.

CHAIN FLOWER

Directory view, page 38

Skill level: Beginner/easy

 Cotton perle in two colours

 5 mm glass seed beads in two colours
1 brooch back for fastening

METHOD

This flower consists of 2 circles in different colours.

First (back) circle: Make 5 ch, sl st in first ch to form a ring.

Round 1: 1 ch, 15 dc in ring, sl st in first dc.

Round 2: *4 ch, sl st in next dc, rep from * to end.

Round 3: sl st in each of first 2 ch of next loop, sl st in centre of same loop, 5 ch, *sl st in centre of next 4-ch loop, 5 ch, rep from * to end, sl st in sl st at centre of first loop.

Round 4: sl st in each of first 3 ch of next loop, sl st in centre of same loop, 6 ch, *sl st in centre of next 5-ch loop, 6 ch, rep from * to end, sl st in sl st at centre of first loop.

Round 5: sl st in each of first 3 ch of next loop, sl st in centre of same loop, 7 ch, *sl st in centre of next 6-ch loop, 7 ch, rep from * to end, sl st in sl st at centre of first loop.

Second (front) circle: Make 5 ch, sl st in first ch to form a ring.

Round 1: 1 ch, 20 dc in ring, sl st in first dc.

Rounds 2–5: Complete as for first circle. Fasten off.

To make up: Place the larger circle over the smaller and stitch the centres together. Thread two separate batches of 10 beads onto thread and sew to the centre of the front circle. Attach to a brooch backing as required.

GOLDEN LEAF

Directory view, page 38

Skill level: Challenging/complex

 Cotton perle

METHOD

Make 5 ch, sl st in first ch to form a ring.

Round 1: 1 dc in ring, *14 ch, 1 tr in 6th ch from hook, (2 ch, miss 2 ch, 1 tr in next ch) twice, 2 ch, 1 dc in ring *, ^ 17 ch, 1 tr in 6th ch from hook, (2 ch, miss 2 ch, 1 tr in next ch) 3 times, 2 ch, 1 dc in ring ^, 20 ch, 1 tr in 6th ch from hook, (2 ch, miss 2 ch, 1 tr in next ch) 4 times, 2 ch, 1 dc in ring, rep from ^ to ^ once and from * to * once.

Round 2: 1 ch, 2 dc in next 2-ch loop, 1 htr in base of next tr, (3 tr in next 2-ch loop, 1 tr in base of next tr), (3 tr in next 2-ch loop, 1 tr, 1 htr in base of next tr), 3 dc in next 5-ch loop, (1 htr, 1 tr) in next tr, (3 tr in next 2-ch loop, 1 tr in next tr), (3 tr in next 2-ch loop, 1 htr in next tr), 2 dc in next 2-ch loop, 1 dc in next dc, (first section of leaf), 2 dc in next 2-ch loop, 1 htr in base of next tr, (3 tr in next 2-ch loop, 1 tr in base of next tr) twice, (3 tr in next 2-ch loop, 1 tr, 1 htr in base of next tr), 3 dc in next 5-ch loop, (1 htr, 1 tr) in next tr, (3 tr in next 2-ch loop, 1 tr in next tr) twice, (3 tr in next 2-ch loop, 1 htr in next tr), 2 dc in next 2-ch loop, 1 dc in next dc, [2nd section of leaf], 2 dc in next 2-ch loop, 1 htr in base of next tr; (3 tr in next 2-ch loop, 1 tr in base of next tr) three times, (3 tr in next 2-ch loop, 1 tr, 1 htr in base of next tr), 3 dc in next 5-ch loop, (1 htr, 1 tr) in next tr, (3 tr in next 2-ch loop, 1 tr in next tr) three times, (3 tr in next 2-ch loop, 1 htr in next tr), 2 dc in next 2-ch loop, 1 dc in next dc, [3rd section of leaf], repeat 2nd section of leaf and then first section of leaf, sl st in first dc.

Round 3: 1 ch, 1 dc in each st all the way round the leaf.

Make stem: 8 ch, 1 dc in 2nd ch from hook, 1 dc in each rem ch, sl st into first ch. Fasten off.

LAZY FROG
Directory view, page 38

Skill level: Beginner/easy

 Cotton perle

 Novelty lazy frog button

METHOD

Make 5 ch, sl st in first ch to form a ring.
Round 1: 1 ch, 10 dc in ring, sl st in first dc.
Round 2: 1 ch, 1 dc in each dc, sl st in first dc.
Round 3: 2 ch, miss 1st dc, 2 htr in each of next 9 dc, 1 htr in first st of round 2, sl st in 2nd of 2 ch.
Round 4: *2 ch, 2 tr in each of next 3 htr; 2 ch, sl st in next htr; rep from * 4 times, placing last st in 2nd of 2 ch on round 2. Fasten off.
Making up: Attach the lazy frog button to the centre of this flower.

 TUFTED FLOWER
Directory view, page 39

Skill level: Beginner/easy

 Cotton perle

 1 brooch back for fastening

METHOD

Make 6 ch, sl st in first ch to form a ring.
Round 1: 1 ch, 20 dc in ring, join with sl st in first ch.
Round 2: 3 ch, 1 tr in same st, 2 tr in each dc to end, sl st in 3rd of 3 ch at beg of round.
Rounds 3–4: As Round 2.
Round 5: 1 ch, 1 dc in each of next 9 sts, insert hook from front to back in next st, miss next 9 sts, insert hook from front to back in next st, yo and draw through first 2 loops on hook, yo and draw through both loops on hook, *1 dc in each of next 10 sts, insert hook from front to back in next st, miss next 9 sts, insert hook from back to front in next st, yo and draw through first 2 loops on hook, yo and draw through both loops on hook, rep from * to end. Fasten off.
To make up: Make the tufted centre by cutting 40 lengths of yarn, each approx 7.5 cm (3 inches) long, firmly bind together around the centre with another piece of yarn. Fold the lengths in half and sew this bound section into the centre of the flower.
Making up: Attach to the brooch backing as required.

CONICAL SHELL
Directory view, page 39

Skill level: Beginner/easy

 Cotton perle

METHOD

Make 29 ch.
Row 1: 2 dc in 2nd ch from hook, 2 dc in next ch, 2 htr in next ch, 2 tr in each of next 22 ch, 2 htr in next ch, 2 dc in last 2 ch. Fasten off.
Twist trim to form a circle and secure with some sewing stitches. This pattern can be made using double trebles to give greater depth.

123 PEARL ROSE
Directory view, page 39

Skill level: Beginner/easy

Cotton perle

4 x 10 mm pearl buttons
1 brooch back for fastening

METHOD

Make 6 ch, sl st in first ch to form a ring.
Round 1: 1 ch, 17 dc in ring, sl st in first ch.
Round 2: 5 ch, miss next 2 dc, *1 dc in next dc, 4 ch, miss next 2 dc, rep from * to end, sl st in 2nd of 5 ch at beg of round.
Round 3: *(1 dc, 1 htr, 5 tr, 1 htr, 1 dc) in next 4-ch loop, rep from * to end, sl st in first dc.
Round 4: *5 ch, pass these chs behind next group of sts, 1 dc in next dc of round 2, inserting the hook from behind, rep from * to end.
Round 5: *(1 dc, 1 htr, 10 tr, 1 htr, 1 dc) in next 5-ch loop, rep from * to end, sl st in first dc.
Round 6: *7 ch, pass these ch behind next group of sts, 1 dc in next dc of round 4, inserting the hook from behind, rep from * to end.

Round 7: *(1 dc, 1 htr, 15 tr, 1 htr, 1 dc) in next 7-ch loop, rep from * to end, sl st in first dc.
Round 8: *8 ch, pass these ch behind next group of sts, 1 dc in next dc of 6th round inserting the hook from behind, rep from * to end.
Round 9: *(1 dc, 1 htr, 5 tr, 10 dtr, 5 tr, 1 htr, 1 dc) in next 7-ch loop, rep from * to end, sl st in first dc. Fasten off.
Making up: Arrange and sew the 4 pearl buttons in the centre of the flower and attach to the brooch backing as required.

124 SNOWFLAKE
Directory view, page 39

Skill level: Beginner/easy

Cotton perle

METHOD

Make 8 ch, sl st in first ch to form a ring.
Round 1: 2 ch, 17 htr in ring, join in top of 2 ch at beg of round.
Round 2: 1 ch, 1 dc in same st, *17 ch, 1 dc in each of next 3 sts, rep from * 5 times, ending last rep with dc in next 2 sts, sl st in first dc.
Round 3: 1 ch, 1 dc in same st, *23 dc in next 17-ch loop, 1 dc in each of next 2 dc, 7 ch, sl st in same dc, 1 dc in next dc, rep from * 5 times, ending last rep with 7 ch, sl st in same tr, sl st in first dc. Fasten off.

ACCESSORIES

SEE ALSO

Standard crochet abbreviations, page 125
Refresher course, pages 110–125

125 RING BUTTON I

Directory view, page 40

Skill level: Beginner/easy

 Cotton perle

 Metal or plastic button ring of the required size

 To fasten into buttonholes on a garment or to add decoration

METHOD

Notes: For this trim you will need a metal or plastic ring of the required size. Always insert the hook into the ring.

Row I: SI st in ring, hold in place, make a ch long enough to reach across the centre area (this will make the bar to sew and secure the button). 3 ch, then tr around half of the ring, hold the securing bar in place, continue to work around the ring until it is completely covered. Fasten off.

126 RING BUTTON 2

Directory view, page 40

Skill level: Beginner/easy

 Cotton perle

Metal or plastic button ring of the required size

 To fasten into buttonholes on a garment or to add decoration

METHOD

Notes: For this trim you will need a metal or plastic ring of the required size. Always insert the hook into the ring.

Row I: SI st into ring, hold in place, make a ch long enough to reach across the centre area (this will make the bar to sew and secure the button). I ch, then dc around half of the ring, hold the securing bar in place, continue to work around the ring until it is completely covered. Fasten off.

 **RING BUTTON 3**
Directory view, page 40

Skill level: Beginner/easy

 Cotton perle

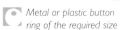 *Metal or plastic button ring of the required size*

To fasten into buttonholes on a garment or to add decoration

METHOD

Notes: For this you need a metal or plastic ring of the required size. Always insert the hook into the ring.

Row 1: Sl st in ring, hold in place, make a ch long enough to reach across the centre area (this will make the bar to sew and secure the button). 1 ch, then dc around half of the ring, hold the securing bar in place, continue to work around the ring until it is completely covered. Do not fasten off.

To complete button: Twist the tops of all the stitches to the inside of the ring and, using a yarn needle, fill in the centre of the button by darning, weaving or using any decorative stitches. Fasten off.

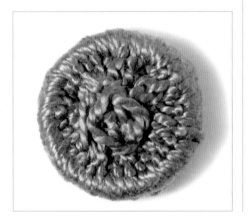

I28 **BALL BUTTON**
Directory view, page 40

Skill level: Beginner/easy

 Cotton perle

To fasten into buttonholes on a garment or to add decoration

METHOD

Notes: The covering for this type of button should be made a little small and the button should be firmly stuffed with yarn or suitable wadding. Make 2 ch.

Round 1: 6 dc in 2nd ch from hook, sl st in first dc.

Round 2: 1 ch, 2 dc in each dc, sl st in first dc.

Round 3: 1 ch, 1 dc in each dc, sl st in first dc. (This completes the first half of this spherical button. Sew in the loose yarn at the beginning of round 1).

Round 4: 1 ch, (1 dc, miss 1 dc) 6 times, sl st in first dc.

Insert some filling material into the centre to pack out the button.

Round 5: 1 ch, (1 dc, miss 1 dc) 3 times, sl st in first dc.

Fasten off leaving sufficient length to close the base of the button and attach it to the garment.

 **COVERED BUTTON**
Directory view, page 40

Skill level: Intermediate

 Cotton perle

 Buttons used: self cover metal button forms

To fasten into buttonholes on a garment or to add decoration

METHOD

Notes: The covering for this type of button should be made a little small, to allow it to stretch to fit the metal button form.

Using a 12.5 cm (5 inch) length of yarn from the ball, wrap this around your finger and ease the circle free.

Round 1: Into this circle work 1 ch, 8 dc, holding firmly in fingers, gently pull the ends of this circle to tighten the ring, join with sl st in first dc.

Round 2: 1 ch, 1 dc in same st, 2 dc in each dc to end, sl st in first dc.

Round 3: 1 ch, *2 dc in next dc, 1 dc in next dc, rep from * to end, sl st in first dc. Increase on following rounds to required size.

Next round: 1 ch, 1 dc in each dc to end, sl st in first dc. Fasten off.

FLORAL BUTTONHOLE
Directory view, page 40

Skill level: Challenging/complex

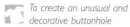 *Cotton perle*   *To create an unusual and decorative buttonhole*

METHOD

Notes: The button forms the centre of the flower. This design suits a wide band.
Make a foundation chain of the required width of button band. You may need to adjust the position of the buttonholes to suit your garment.
Row 1: 1 ch, 1 dc in each st to end, turn. Work as many rows of dc as required.
Buttonhole row: Place buttonholes as required, by making 2 ch, miss 2 dc, near the centre of the width of the band.
Next row: Work in dc, with 2 dc in the 2-chain loop.
Repeat the buttonhole row, next row and rows of dc to suit your garment, end with a few rows of dc. Fasten off

Flower: Ensure the centre opening will fit comfortably over the button and around the buttonhole.
Make the required number of ch, sl st in first ch to form ring.
Round 1: 1 ch, make an even number of dc in the ring (the exact number will be determined by the size of your buttonhole).
Round 2: 3 ch, 1 tr in next dc, *3 ch, 1 tr in each of next 2 sts, rep from * to end, 3 ch, sl st in top of 3 ch. Fasten off.
Sew ring of flower around buttonhole.

 **STANDARD BUTTONHOLES**
Directory view, page 41

Skill level: Intermediate

 Cotton Perle *To fasten with buttons on a garment or to add decoration*

METHOD

Make a foundation chain of the required length or work row 1 directly into the garment fabric. You may need to adjust the position of the first buttonhole you work to suit your garment.
Row 1: 1 ch, 1 dc in each st to end, turn. Work as many rows of dc as required.
Buttonhole Row: (Based on 9 stitch width) 2 ch, 3 tr, *1 ch, miss 1 dc, 4 tr, rep from * to end.
Final row: Work 1 more row of dc, placing 1 dc into each 1-ch loop. Fasten off.

132 CLOSE BUTTONHOLES

Directory view, page 41

Skill level: Intermediate

 Cotton perle

 To fasten with buttons on a garment or to add decoration

METHOD

Make a foundation chain of the required length, or work row 1 directly into the item to be trimmed with right side facing.
Row 1: 1 ch, 1 dc in each st to end, turn. You may need to adjust the placement of the buttonholes to suit your garment. The sample was worked as stated below and using a contrasting colour.
Work as many rows of dc as required.
Buttonhole row: 1 ch, 1 dc, *2 ch, miss 2 dc, 1 dc in next dc, rep from * to end.
Final row: Work 1 more row of dc, placing 2 dc in each 2-ch loop. Fasten off.

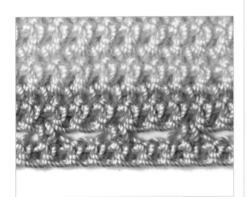

133 LOOP BUTTONHOLES

Directory view, page 41

Skill level: Beginner/easy

 Cotton perle

 To fasten with buttons on a garment or to add decoration

METHOD

Make a foundation chain of the required length, or work row 1 directly into the item to be trimmed with right side facing.
Row 1: 1 ch, 1 dc in each st to end, turn. Work as many rows of dc as required.
Place chain loops on the buttonhole row to suit your garment. The sample was worked as stated below and using a contrasting colour.
Buttonhole row: 1 ch, 2 dc, *3 ch, 1 dc in each of next 4 dc, rep from * to end. Fasten off.

134 CURVED BUTTONHOLES

Directory view, page 41

Skill level: Intermediate

 Cotton perle

 To fasten with buttons on a garment or to add decoration

METHOD

Make a foundation chain of the required length, or work row 1 directly into the item to be trimmed with right side facing.
Before starting decide how many buttonholes are required. Space them evenly over the opening band. To suit your garment, you may need to adjust the number of dc between the 5-ch loops on row 3. The sample was worked with 8 dc between the button holes, giving a multiple of 9 stitches.
Row 1: 1 ch, 1 dc in each st to end, turn.
Row 2: As row 1.
Row 3: 1 ch, 1 dc in first dc, 1 dc in each of next 3 dc, *5 ch, miss 1 dc, 1 dc in each of next 8 dc, rep from * to end, ending last rep with 4 dc, turn.
Row 4: 1 ch, 1 dc in first dc, 1 dc in next dc, *miss 2 dc, (2 ch, 1 tr in 5-ch loop) 4 times, 2 ch, miss 2 dc, 1 dc in each of next 4 dc, rep from * ending last rep with 2 dc. Fasten off.

LOOPED PICOT BUTTONHOLES

Directory view, page 42

Skill level: Intermediate

 Cotton perle 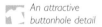 *An attractive buttonhole detail*

METHOD

Notes: Picot = 3 ch, I dc in Ist ch.
Before starting decide how many buttonholes are required. Space them evenly over the opening band. To suit your garment, you may need to adjust the number of dc between the 9-ch loops on row 4. The edging is shown in green in the photograph.
Make a foundation chain of the required length, or work row 1 directly into the item to be trimmed with right side facing. (multiple of 8 stitches + 5)
Row I: I ch, I dc in each st to end, turn.
Row 2: As row I.
Row 3: As row I.
Row 4: I ch, miss Ist dc, I dc in each of next 4 dc, *9 ch, miss 3 dc, I dc in each of next 5 dc, rep from * to end, turn.
Row 5: I ch, miss Ist dc, I dc in each of next 3 dc, *5 ch, I dc in 9-ch loop, picot, I dc in 9-ch loop, 5 ch, miss I dc, I dc in each of next 3 dc, rep from * to last st, I dc.
Fasten off.

 PICOT BUTTONHOLES

Directory view, page 42

Skill level: Intermediate

 Cotton perle   *To fasten with buttons on a garment or to add decoration*

METHOD

Notes: Picot = 3 ch, sl st into 3rd ch from hook.
Make a foundation chain of the required length, or work row 1 directly into the item to be trimmed with right side facing.
Row I: I ch, I dc in each st to end, turn.
Work as many rows of dc as required. Place chain loops on the buttonhole row to suit your garment.
Buttonhole row I: I ch, 2 dc, *3 ch, miss 3 dc, 4 dc, rep from * to end.
Next row: Work in dc, with 3 dc in each chain loop.
Final row: I ch, *dc to centre dc of next buttonhole, I picot, rep from * to end.
Fasten off.

 TEXTURED RUFFLE

Directory view, page 42

Skill level: Challenging/complex

Cotton perle *This is such a dense and textured piece of crochet it will give decorative contrast to any garment*

METHOD

This is formed by working many treble crochets into a small space on a background fabric of treble crochet to give a fluted effect.
Make a foundation chain of the required length.
Row I: I dtr in 5th ch from hook, I dtr into each ch to end, turn.
Row 2: 4 ch, I dtr into each st to end, DO NOT TURN.
Row 3: 3 ch, work 6 tr down stem of first dtr, I tr into st at base of this st, *7 tr up stem of next dtr in row, I tr into top of this st, 7 tr down stem of next dtr in row, I tr into st at base of this dtr, rep from * to end of row. Fasten off.
Repeat row 3 on the first row that was worked.

DIAMONDS INSERTION
Directory view, page 42

Skill level: Intermediate

 Cotton perle   *An insertion or link allowing two pieces of fabric to be joined together to lengthen a skirt or sleeves*

METHOD

To make one diamond:
Row 1: 5 ch, sl st in first ch to form a ring, 1 ch, 1 dc in ring, 3 ch, 1 htr in ring, turn.
Row 2: 5 ch, 1 dc in first 3-ch loop, 3 ch (1 dc, 3 ch, 1 htr) in last 3-ch loop, turn.
Row 3: 5 ch, 1 dc in first 3-ch loop, (3 ch, 1 tr in next 3-ch loop) to last 3-ch loop, (3 ch, 1 dc, 3 ch,1 htr) in last 3-ch loop, turn.
Rep row 3 until the diamond is the required size.
Next Row: 3 ch, miss first 3-ch loop, 1 dc in next 3-ch loop (3 ch, 1 dc in next 3-ch loop) to last 3-ch loop, turn.
Rep this row the same number of times row 3 was repeated.
Final Row: 3 ch, miss next 3-ch loop, 1 htr into last ch sp. Fasten off.

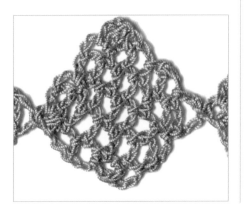

 DECORATIVE CUFF
Directory view, page 43

Skill level: Challenging/complex

 Cotton perle   *Lengthen a sleeve with this decorative cuff*

METHOD

Notes: tr2tog = work 1 tr in each of next 2 tr until 1 loop of each remains on hook, yo and draw through all 3 loops on hook.
Main section:
Make a foundation chain of the required length, or work row 1 directly into the item to be trimmed with right side facing. (multiple of 4 stitches + 3)
Row 1: 2 ch, *tr2tog over next 2 sts, 1 ch, rep from * to last 2 sts, tr2tog, turn.
Row 2: 3 ch, *tr2tog in next 1-ch loop, 1 ch, rep from * to last 2 sts, tr2tog, turn.
Rep row 2 to the desired length. Do not fasten off, continue with frill section.

Frill section:
Row 1: *5 ch, sl st in top of next tr2tog, rep from * to end, turn.
Row 2: 3 ch, (2 tr, 3 ch, 3 tr) in first 5-ch loop, *2 ch, sl st in next 5-ch loop, 2 ch, 3 tr, 3 ch, 3 tr in next 5-ch loop, rep from * to end, turn.
Row 3: 1 ch, *1 dc in each st to next 3-ch loop, 5 dc in 3-ch loop, rep from * to last 3 sts, 3 dc, turn.
Row 4: 3 ch, 1 tr in each of next 4 dc, *2 tr in each of next 3 dc, 1 tr in each of next 13 dc, rep from * ending last rep with 1 tr in each of next 3 dc, 1 tr in the top of the turning ch. Fasten off.

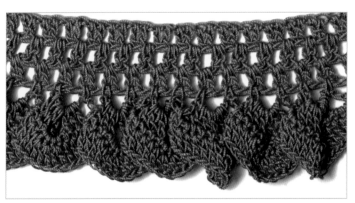

140 COLUMNS INSERTION
Directory view, page 43

Skill level: Beginner/easy

 Cotton perle

 An insertion or link allowing two pieces of fabric to be joined together to lengthen a skirt or sleeves

METHOD

Make a foundation chain of the required length or work row 1 directly into the item to be trimmed with right side facing. (any number of stitches)
Row 1: 1 ch, 1 dc in each ch to end, turn.
Row 2: 4 ch, 1 dtr in each dc to end.
Row 3: As row 1.

141 SPIKED COLUMNS INSERTION
Directory view, page 43

Skill level: Intermediate

 Cotton perle in two colours

 An insertion or link allowing two pieces of fabric to be joined together to lengthen a skirt or sleeves

METHOD

Notes: There is no right or wrong side, it depends which looks best on the garment. Make a ch of the required length or work row 1 directly into the item to be trimmed. (any number of stitches)
Row 1: 1 ch, 1 dc in each ch to end, turn.
Row 2: 2 ch, 1 dtr in each dc to end.
Row 3: As row 1. Fasten off.
With a contrasting yarn and a larger hook, work loose sl sts along the centre of row 2, as shown in the picture. Fasten off.

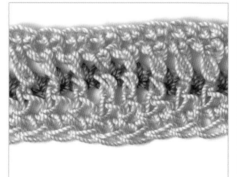

142 MINI CIRCLES INSERTION
Directory view, page 43

Skill level: Beginner/easy

 Cotton perle

To either add texture and interest or to use as an insertion or link allowing two pieces of fabric to be joined together to lengthen a skirt or sleeves

METHOD

Make 5 ch, sl st in first ch to form a ring.
Row 1: 1 ch, 8 dc in ring, sl st in first dc, turn.
Row 2: 1 ch, 2 dc in each dc, sl st in first dc. Fasten off.

BASIC COLLAR
Directory view, page 44

Skill level: Intermediate

 Cotton perle   *To add interest to any garment neckline or to a cushion*

METHOD

Make a foundation chain of the required length, or work row I directly into the item to be trimmed with right side facing. (multiple of 3 stitches)
Row I: I ch, I dc in each st to end, turn.
Row 2: As row I.
Row 3: 2 ch, I tr in each dc to end, turn.
Row 4: 2 ch, *(I tr, I dtr, I tr) in next tr, 2 tr, rep from * to end, omitting I tr at end of last rep, turn.
Row 5: *3 ch, I dc in next dtr, rep from * to end, ending with 2 ch, dc in last st. Fasten off.

 LACE COLLAR
Directory view, page 44

Skill level: Challenging/complex

 Cotton perle   *To add some interest to any garment neckline or to a cushion*

METHOD

Notes: tr2tog = work I tr into each of next 2 tr until I loop of each remains on hook, yo and draw through all 3 loops on hook. Make a foundation chain of the required length, or work row I directly into the item to be trimmed with right side facing. (multiple of 9 stitches + 4)
Row I: I ch, I dc in each st to end, turn.
Row 2: I ch, I dc in first dc, 2 ch, miss 2 dc, I dc in next dc, *miss 2 dc, 6 tr in next dc, miss 2 dc, I dc in next dc, 2 ch, miss 2 dc, I dc in next dc, rep from * to end, turn.

Row 3: I ch, I dc in first dc, 2 ch, *I tr in next tr, I ch, I tr in next tr 5 times, I dc in next 2 ch sp, rep from * to last 3 sts, omitting I dc at end of last rep, 2 ch, I dc in last dc.
Row 4: 3 ch, (I tr in next tr, 2 ch) 4 times, *tr2tog, 2 ch, (I tr in next tr, 2 ch) 4 times, rep from * to last tr, tr2tog over next tr and dc at end of row. Fasten off.

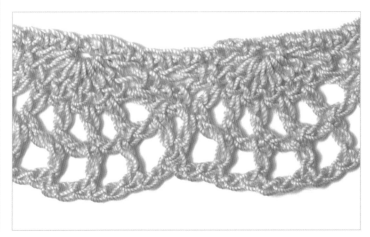

145 INTRICATE LACE COLLAR
Directory view, page 44

Skill level: Challenging/complex

 Cotton perle

 To add some interest to any garment neckline or to a cushion

METHOD

Make a foundation chain of the required length, or work row 1 directly into the item to be trimmed with right side facing. (multiple of 11 stitches)

Row 1: 1 ch, 1 dc in each st to end, turn.

Row 2: 5 ch, 1 tr in 4th dc, *2 ch, miss 1 dc, 1 tr in next dc, rep from * to end, turn.

Row 3: 3 ch, *1 tr in next 2-ch loop, 2 ch, rep from * to last 2-ch loop, 1 tr in loop, 1 tr in top of turning chain, turn.

Row 4: 5 ch, *1 tr in next 2-ch loop, 2 ch, rep from * to end, 1 tr in top of turning ch, turn.

Row 5: 1 ch, 1 dc in first st, 1 dc in next 2-ch loop, *5 ch, 1 dc in next 2-ch loop, 1 dc in next tr, 11 ch, 1 dtr in 8th ch from hook, 1 dtr in next 2 ch, 1 dtr in last dc worked into, miss next 2-ch loop, 1 dc in next tr, 1 dc in next ch loop, 5 ch, 1 dc in next tr, rep from * to last 2-ch loop, 2 dc in loop, turn.

Row 6: 5 ch, *10 dc in next 7-ch loop, 5 ch, 1 dc in 5-ch loop, 1 dc in next 5-ch loop, rep from * to end, working final dc in last st. Fasten off.

146 FAN COLLAR
Directory view, page 44

Skill level: Beginner/easy

 Cotton perle

 To add some interest to any garment neckline or to a cushion

METHOD

Main section:
Make a foundation chain of 7 stitches, turn.

Row 1: 3 tr in 6th ch from hook, 2 ch, 3 tr in next ch, turn.

Row 2: 5 ch, (3 tr, 2 ch, 3 tr) in 2-ch loop, *1 tr in top of turning ch, turn.

Row 3: 3 ch, (3 tr, 2 ch, 3 tr) in 2-ch sp, turn.

Rep rows 2 and 3 until straight edge fits around neck, ending on row 2, work last repeat of row 2 to *, 2 ch, 1 tr in 2-ch loop at end of previous row. Fasten off.

Inner edging:
Position collar so shells point towards the centre front, rejoin yarn to straight edge: 1 ch, 2 tr into each sp along edge.
Fasten off.

Outer edging:
On RS rejoin yarn into 5-ch loop at edge of collar, 3 ch, 8 tr in same loop, 9 tr in each 5-ch loop to end, work 1 tr in the 2-ch loop or between 3 tr groups at end of last row of main section of collar.
Fasten off.

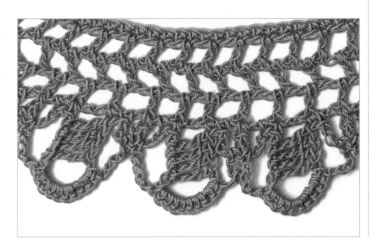

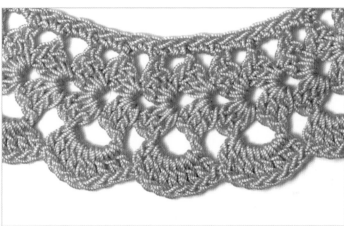

 **PICOT COLLAR**
Directory view, page 44

Skill level: Beginner/easy

 Cotton perle   To add an attractive collar to a garment neckline

METHOD

Make a foundation chain of the required length, or work row 1 directly into the item to be trimmed with right side facing. (multiple of 7 stitches)
Row 1: 1 ch, 1 dc in 2nd ch from hook, 1 dc in each of next 5 ch, *turn, 7 ch, miss 5 dc, 1 dc in next dc, turn, (6 dc, 5 ch, 6 dc) in 7-ch loop,1 dc in next 6 foundation ch, rep from * to end, omitting 6 dc at end of last rep.

 RINGS BELT
Directory view, page 45

Skill level: Beginner/easy

 Cotton perle   To make an attractive and unusual belt
 5 circular craft rings A length of fine braid to link the covered rings together

METHOD

The belt shown uses five rings in leaf green. Each ring is covered in the same way.
Make a slip knot in the usual way and work dc into a plastic craft ring as if you were working into a chain ring: covering the ring completely. Ensure that the stitches are pushed closely together to fully cover the ring when the belt is worn. Fasten off and sew in all the yarn ends.
Place the rings in three layers as shown in the photograph and weave the braid through them. You may make more groups to use around the belt.
Secure the ends of the braid with a few stitches.

149 DOUBLE RINGS BELT
Directory view, page 45

Skill level: Beginner/easy

 Cotton perle in two contrasting shades

 To make an attractive and unusual belt

 *7 circular craft rings
A length of fine decorative braid to link the covered rings together*

METHOD

The belt shown uses four rings in jade green and three rings in sage green. Each ring is covered in the same way.

Make a slip knot in the usual way and work dc into a plastic craft ring as if you were working into a chain ring: covering the ring completely. Ensure that the stitches are pushed closely together to fully cover the ring when the belt is worn. Fasten off and sew in all the yarn ends.

Place the rings in two layers as shown in the photograph and weave the braid through them. You may make more groups of covered rings to use around the belt.

Secure the ends of the braid with a few stitches.

150 BEADED BELT TIE
Directory view, page 45

Skill level: Beginner/easy

 Cotton perle in two colours: A and B

To add decoration to a belt

5 mm glass seed beads

METHOD

Make a dc belt 5–10 cm (2–4 inches) wide and to the required length. This can be worked as a few rows of the required length or as a large number of rows of required depth. You may need to make more lengths of chain for the tie if your belt is wider than the 5-cm (2-inch) width shown.

Tie detail: Decide on the finished length of tie. For each end of the belt, make 2 lengths of chain in the yarn used to make the belt (yarn A) and 4 lengths in a contrasting colour (yarn B).

Arrange the chains in the following order: B A B B A B, fold in two and sew in place, using the picture as a guide.

Slide 3 beads onto each length of chain and tie a small knot at the end to secure beads in place. Tie a second knot at the top of these beads. Sew in the yarn ends.

PROJECTS

The five projects in this chapter are designed to provide ideas and inspiration for using the trims in the directory. As well as looking at how the trims can be applied to existing garments and soft furnishings the projects also demonstrate how varying the yarns and beads used in the directory can bring a whole new look to the trims.

PROJECT 1

Skill level: Beginner/easy

Trim used: 128 Ball button

YOU WILL NEED

- Child's cardigan
- Chunky cotton yarn in coordinating colours, here strawberry pink and peachy orange are used
- Washable wadding to stuff the ball buttons
- 3.5 mm crochet hook

BOBBLE BOLERO

This classic pink bolero for a little girl has been made into a party piece by attaching dangling ball buttons to the hem and as a button. The crochet on these hanging buttons is chunky and fun. The buttons have been filled with wadding to give greater volume and interest without adding weight. A bright orange trim has also been added to the garment edge.

GARMENT EDGE

Starting at the left-hand edge opposite the buttonhole with right side of garment facing, work 1 row of sl st in orange around the lower edge of the ribbing – 147 ch. Work 23 ch around the buttonhole to form a circle about 5 mm (³⁄₁₆ inch) out from the buttonhole edge. Fasten off. You may need to adjust the number of stitches around the hem of the bolero to suit the garment you are working on.

WORKING THE BALL BUTTON

Using the pattern for the Ball button (trim 128), make seven buttons in pink and seven in orange. You will also need to make a slightly smaller pink button for the buttonhole.

Note: The covering for this type of button should be made a little small and the button should be firmly stuffed with washable wadding or yarn.

Make 2 ch.
Round 1: 6 dc in 2nd ch from hook, sl st in first sc.
Round 2: 1 ch, 2 dc in each dc, sl st in first dc.
Round 3: 1 ch, 1 dc in each dc, sl st in first dc. (This completes the first half of this spherical button. Sew in the loose yarn at the beginning of round 1).
Round 4: 1 ch, (1 dc, miss 1 dc) 6 times, sl st in first dc.
Insert some yarn or washable wadding into the centre to pack out the button.
Round 5: 1 ch, (1 dc, miss 1 dc) 3 times, sl st in first dc.

Fasten off leaving at least 10 cm (4 inches) of yarn to close the base of the button (after stuffing) and attach it to the garment.

FINISHING

Make three evenly spaced knots of the length of yarn left on the buttons. With a yarn needle sew the buttons to the orange sl st row on the jacket at regular intervals, alternating the colours.

TRY THIS

You could try using a fine yarn to make clusters of two or three hanging bobbles or you could try arranging some more bobbles around the body of the cardigan.

PROJECT 2

Skill level: Intermediate

Trim used: 28 Posy Edge

YOU WILL NEED

- Wrap-around cardigan
- Yarn: Fingering weight merino/cashmere mixture in coordinating colours, here spring green is used
- 3.5 mm crochet hook

POSY-EDGED CARDIGAN

This lightweight wrap-around cardigan has been greatly enhanced by the posy edge, which has been hand-sewn to the neckline and to the sleeve edges. Worked in a soft and delicate fingering-weight, merino/cashmere yarn, this intricate edging creates a refreshing and elegant effect.

WORKING THE POSY EDGE

Using the pattern for trim 28, Posy Edge, work the following:
A length of 22 motifs for neck edge – length 72 cm (28 inches).
A length of 10 motifs for each of the sleeve edges – length 31 cm (12 inches).

Note: You may need to adjust the number of motifs if the size of your garment is different to the one shown in the picture. As there is no foundation chain for this edging, this is very easy to achieve.

There is no foundation chain for this edging.
Row 1: 4 ch, 1 tr in 4th ch from hook (centre ring made), (3 ch, 2 tr into ring, 3 ch, 1 sl st in ring) 3 times (3 petals made = 1 motif), *11 ch, 1 tr into 4th ch from hook, 3 ch, 1 tr in ring, 1 sl st between 2 tr of last petal made, 1 tr into ring, 3 ch, 1 sl st in ring, (3 ch, 2 tr in ring, 3 ch, 1 sl st in ring) twice, rep from * to length required. Fasten off.

PATTERN VARIATION

To finish the tapering neckline, rejoin yarn to each end in turn, 1 tr, 2 dc. Fasten off.

FINISHING

Pin the edgings into position and hand sew with a matching thread using back stitch or any basic, small, neat stitch.

TRY THIS

To achieve a formal evening look you could try using a silky yarn in deep green for the posy trim. You could also stitch beads around the centre of the posies.

PROJECT 3

Skill level: Challenging/complex

Trims used: 45 Curlicue fringe
124 Snowflake

YOU WILL NEED

- Silk cushion cover, 45 x 45 cm (18 x 18 inches)
- Yarn A: Sport weight wool/cotton mixture in a coordinating colour, here burnt orange is used
- Yarn B: Fingering weight wool/nylon mixture in coordinating variegated shades, here autumnal shades are used
- 3 mm crochet hook

FRILLED CUSHION

This rich mixture of autumnal shades lends a special texture to a plain orange cushion cover. The fringe is worked with random spacing between the curlicues, allowing for a certain amount of personal creativity in the project, it also allows for any variation in the lengths of the cushion edges. The motif, on the other hand, provides a contrast with its uniform and structured appearance.

WORKING THE CURLICUE FRINGE

First section
Using yarn A, (leave a long end, in case you need to adjust the length) make a length of chain to fit just inside the edge of the cushion cover, plus twelve chains.
(multiple of 4 stitches + 1)
1 dc in 2nd ch, *1 dc in each ch to the next corner of the cushion cover, miss 3 ch, rep from * to end, fasten off. Do not join the ends of the strip together at this stage, it will be easier to work the second section.

Second section
Use yarn B to complete the fringe.
Row 1: Join yarn to the opposite side of the foundation chain, with the same side of the work facing as for the first section, work one row of dc, including working 1 dc in each of the ch missed on the first section, turn.
Row 2: 2 ch, *1 htr in each st to the next corner, 3 htr in centre of corner, rep from * to end, turn.
Row 3: As row 2.

Row 4: 1 ch, *3 dc (see pattern variation below), ^9 ch, 4 dc in 3rd ch from hook, (4 tr in next ch) 6 times, 1 sl st in last dc worked on fringe header ^, rep from ^ to ^ once, rep from * to end. Fasten off.

PATTERN VARIATION

Row 4: 3, 4 or 5 dc were randomly worked between each curlicue to provide a relaxed and laid back appearance.

Corner details: work one curlicue 2 or 3 sts either side of each corner and one curlicue directly on the corner.

Note: Leave the ends of yarn at the beginning and the end of this fringe, as they can be used to weave the two edges together after the fringe has been sewn onto the cushion cover.

WORKING THE SNOWFLAKE

Using Yarn A, and the 3 mm crochet
hook make 8 ch, sl st in first ch to
form a ring.

Round 1: 2 ch, 17 htr in ring, join in
top of 2 ch at beg of round.

Round 2: 1 ch, 1 dc in same st,
*17 ch, 1 dc in each of next 3 sts,
rep from * 5 times, ending last rep
with dc in next 2 sts, sl st in first dc.

Round 3: 1 ch, 1 dc in same st, *23 dc
in next 17-ch loop, 1 dc in each of
next 2 dc, 7 ch, sl st in same dc, 1 dc
in next dc, rep from * 5 times, ending
last rep with 7 ch, sl st in same tr, sl st
in first dc. Fasten off.

FINISHING

Attach the fringe and motif to the
cushion cover by pinning into position
and then hand-sewing with a matching
thread using back stitch or any small,
neat stitch. Join the ends of the fringe
and fasten off all ends.

TRY THIS

An alternative way to
work the fringing on this
cushion is to have double
or triple rows of fringing
worked in contrasting
textures and colours.

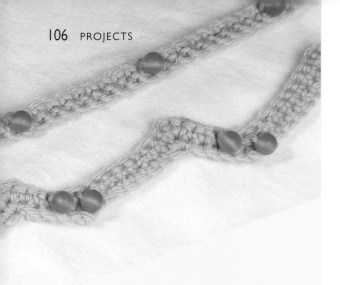

DOUBLE-TRIMMED SKIRT

Adding two different crochet braids to this basic white skirt adds interest and texture to a plain garment. Position the braids so that there is a gap between them suitable to allow them to interact visually.

PROJECT 4

Skill level: Intermediate

Trims used: 76 Jazzy braid (top)
              86 Angled chevrons (bottom)

YOU WILL NEED

- Basic white cotton skirt
- Fingering weight merino/cashmere mixture yarn in a complementary colour, here spring green is used
- 67 5 mm matte glass beads (25 beads for the upper trim and 42 for the lower trim) in a colour complementary or toning to the yarn, here pink is used
- 3.5 mm crochet hook

FINISHED SIZE

Trim 76, Jazzy braid, the upper trim, is 114 cm (45 inches) long.
Trim 86, Angled chevrons, the lower trim, is 120 cm (47 inches) long.

WORKING THE UPPER TRIM (JAZZY BRAID)

Thread 25 beads onto the yarn before starting work.
Make a foundation chain of the required length.
(multiple of 10 stitches + 1)
Row 1: 1 dc in 2nd ch from hook, 1 dc in each ch to end, turn.
Row 2: 1 ch, working along the opposite side of the foundation chain, *bring down a bead to work into next dc, 9 dc, rep from * to end. Fasten off.

WORKING THE LOWER TRIM (ANGLED CHEVRONS)

Thread 42 beads onto the yarn before starting work.
Make a foundation chain of the required length.
(multiple of 14 stitches + 2)
Row 1: 1 ch, 2 dc in second ch from hook, *1 dc in each of next 8 ch, miss 1 ch, 1 dc in each of next 4 ch, 3 tr in next ch, rep from * to end, omitting 1 dc at end of last rep, turn.
Row 2: 1 ch, 2 dc in first dc, *1 dc into each of next 3 dc, bring down 1 bead to work into next dc, miss 1 dc, bring down 1 bead to work into next dc, 1 dc in each of next 8 dc, 3 dc in next ch, rep from * to last long section of chevron, end with 2 dc in last st. Fasten off.

FINISHING

Pin the trims into position and hand-sew with a matching thread using back stitch or any basic, small, neat stitch.

TRY THIS

If you wanted to trim a winter skirt you could try using a chunkier DK yarn with larger beads. Alternatively, you could try making one or two more additional trims to add interest and texture.

PROJECT 5

Skill level: Beginner/easy

Trim used: 123 Pearl rose
98 Irish leaf

YOU WILL NEED

❧ Beret

❧ Sport weight cotton yarn in a complementary colour, here pink and burnt orange are used

❧ 5 1 cm heart-shaped pearl beads in a coordinating colour for the centre of the rose, here pink beads are used

❧ 3.5 mm crochet hook

EMBELLISHED BERET

These charming motifs are simple, quick and fun to make and they are great for embellishing any item of clothing. The large two-coloured flower and Irish leaf used in this project add a bold, fun detail to this beret.

WORKING THE IRISH LEAF

Work the leaf motif in pink with a total of 6 rows.
Note: Work into back loop only on each repeat of row 2.
Make 11 ch.
Row 1: Working into one loop only along first side of ch, 1 dc in 2nd ch from hook, 1 dc in each of next 8 ch, 3 dc in last ch, working in one loop only along other side of foundation ch, 1 dc into each of next 7 ch, turn.
Row 2: Working in back loop only, 1 ch, 1 dc in first dc, 1 dc in each of next 7 dc, 3 dc in next dc, 1 dc in each of next 7 dc, turn.
Rep row 2 as many times as desired. Fasten off.

WORKING THE PEARL ROSE

Notes: Work rounds 1–3 in pink, rounds 4–7 in burnt orange and rounds 8–9 in pink.
Make 6 ch, sl st in 1 ch to form a ring.
Round 1: 1 ch, 17 dc in ring, sl st in first ch.
Round 2: 5 ch, miss next 2 dc, *1 dc in next dc, 4 ch, miss next 2 dc, rep from * to end, sl st in 2nd of 5 ch at beg of round.
Round 3: *(1 dc, 1 htr, 5 tr, 1 htr, 1 dc) in next 4-ch loop, rep from * to end, sl st in first dc.

Round 4: *5 ch, pass these ch behind next group of sts, 1 dc in next dc of round 2, inserting the hook from behind, rep from * to end.
Round 5: *(1 dc, 1 htr, 10 tr, 1 htr, 1 dc) in next 5-ch loop, rep from * to end, sl st in first dc.
Round 6: *7 ch, pass these ch behind next group of sts, 1 dc in next dc of round 4, inserting the hook from behind, rep from * to end.
Round 7: *(1 dc, 1 htr, 15 tr, 1 htr, 1 dc) in next 7-ch loop, rep from * to end, sl st in first dc.
Round 8: *8 ch, pass these ch behind next group of sts, 1 dc in next dc of 6th round inserting the hook from behind, rep from * to end.
Round 9: *(1 dc, 1 htr, 5 tr, 10 dtr, 5 tr, 1 htr, 1 dc) in next 7-ch loop, rep from * to end, sl st in first dc. Fasten off.
Making up: Arrange and sew the heart-shaped pearl beads in the centre of the flower.

FINISHING

Pin the motifs into position on the beret and hand sew with a matching thread using back stitch or any basic, small, neat stitch.

TRY THIS

For a different effect, try using a fine yarn for the centre rounds of the motif and a thicker, chunkier yarn for the outer two rounds.

REFRESHER COURSE

This Refresher Course in crochet skills will guide you through everything you need to make all of the trims in this book. Information is supplied on all the fundamentals from choosing hook and yarn and working basic stitches, to working textured stitches, working in the round and adding beads and sequins.

MATERIALS AND EQUIPMENT

Crochet is one of the easiest crafts to take up because you need very little initial equipment: just a ball of yarn and a crochet hook. Other accessories, such as pins and sharp scissors, are useful and relatively inexpensive.

YARNS

There are a huge range of yarns available to use for crochet, from very fine cotton to chunky wool. Yarns can be made from one fibre or combine a mixture of two or three different ones. As a general rule, the easiest yarns to use for crochet have a smooth surface and a medium or tight twist.

Woollen yarns and blended yarns with a high proportion of wool feel good to crochet with as they have a certain amount of stretch, making it easy to push the point of the hook into each stitch. Silk yarn has a delightful lustre, but it has less resilience than either wool or cotton and is much more expensive. Yarns made from cotton and linen are durable and cool to wear, and may be blended with other fibres to add softness. Yarns made wholly from synthetic fibres, such as acrylic or nylon, are usually less expensive to buy than those made from natural fibres, but can pill when worn and lose their shape. A good solution is to choose a yarn with a small proportion of synthetic fibres that has been combined with a natural fibre, such as wool or cotton.

Yarn is sold by weight, rather than by length, although the packaging of many yarns now includes the length per ball as well as the weight.

HOOKS

Crochet hooks are available in a wide range of sizes, shapes and materials. The most common sorts of hooks are made from aluminium or plastic. Small sizes of steel hooks are also made for working crochet with very fine cotton yarns. Hand-made wooden, bamboo and horn hooks are also available, many featuring decorative handles.

There appears to be no standardization of hook sizing between manufacturers. The points and throats of different brands of hooks often vary in shape which affects the size of stitch they produce.

Hook sizes are quoted differently in Europe and the United States and some brands of hooks are labelled with more than one type of numbering. Choosing a hook is largely a matter of personal preference.

The hook sizes quoted in pattern instructions are a very useful guide, but you may find that you need to use smaller or larger hook sizes, depending on the brand, to achieve the correct tension for a pattern. The most important thing to consider when choosing a hook is how it feels in your hand and the ease with which it works with your yarn. When you have found your perfect brand of hook, it's useful to buy a range of several different sizes.

USEFUL HOOK/YARN COMBINATIONS
Sport weight (4ply) 2.5–3.5 mm (B–E)
Double knitting (DK) 3.5–4.5 mm (E–G)
Worsted weight (Aran) 5–6 mm (I–J)

METRIC/US EQUIVALENTS
28 g = 1 oz
50 g = 1¾ oz
57 g = 2 oz
100 g = 3½ oz
2.5 cm = 1 inch
10 cm = 4 inches
91.4 cm = 1 yard
1 m = 39½ inches

YARN TYPES AND WEIGHTS

Yarns are available in a range of weights varying from very fine to very bulky. Although each weight of yarn is described by a specific name, as shown in the samples below, there may actually be a lot of variation in the thicknesses when yarns are produced by different manufacturers or in different countries.

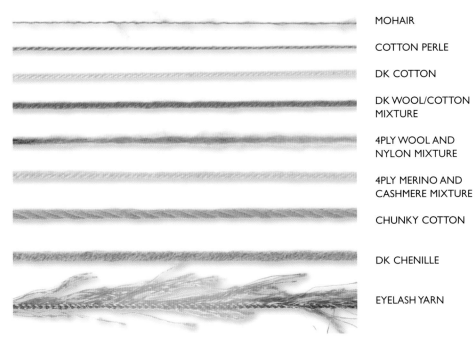

MOHAIR

COTTON PERLE

DK COTTON

DK WOOL/COTTON MIXTURE

4PLY WOOL AND NYLON MIXTURE

4PLY MERINO AND CASHMERE MIXTURE

CHUNKY COTTON

DK CHENILLE

EYELASH YARN

ADDITIONAL EQUIPMENT

TAPE MEASURE
Choose one that shows both centimetres and inches on the same side and replace when it becomes worn or frayed.

MARKERS
Split rings or shaped loops can be used to mark a place on a pattern, to indicate the beginning row of a repeat, and to help with counting the stitches on the foundation chain.

YARN NEEDLES
Yarn needles come in a range of sizes and are used for weaving in yarn ends and for sewing pieces of crochet together.

PINS
Glass-headed pins are the best type to use for blocking. Quilters' long pins with fancy heads are useful when pinning pieces of crochet together as the heads are easy to see and won't slip through the crochet fabric.

ROW COUNTER
A knitter's row counter will help you keep track of the number of rows you have worked, or you may prefer to use a notebook and pencil.

SHARP SCISSORS
Choose a small, pointed pair to cut yarn and trim off yarn ends.

COMPARATIVE CROCHET HOOK SIZES (FROM SMALLEST TO LARGEST)					
STEEL			ALUMINIUM OR PLASTIC		
UK	US	METRIC (MM)	UK	US	METRIC (MM)
6	14	0.60	14		2.00
5½	13		13		
5	12	0.75	12	B	2.50
4½	11		11	C	3.00
4	10	1.00	10	D	
3½	9		9	E	3.50
3	8	1.25	8	F	4.00
2½	7	1.50	7	G	4.50
2	6	1.75	6	H	5.00
1½	5		5	I	5.50
1	4	2.00	4	J	6.00
1/0	3		2	K	7.00
2/0	2	2.50			
3/0	1	3.00			
	0				
	00	3.5			

BASIC SKILLS

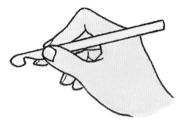 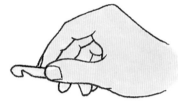

HOLDING THE HOOK AND YARN

1 Holding the hook as if it was a pen is the most widely used method. Centre the tips of your right thumb and forefinger over the flat section of the hook.

2 An alternative way to hold the hook is to grasp the flat section of the hook between your right thumb and forefinger as if you were holding a knife.

3 To control the supply and keep an even tension on the yarn, loop the short end of the yarn over your left forefinger and take the yarn coming from the ball loosely around the little finger on the same hand. Use the middle finger on the same hand to help hold the work. If left-handed, hold the hook in the left hand and the yarn in the right.

WORKING A FOUNDATION CHAIN

The foundation chain is the equivalent of casting on in knitting and it's important to make sure that you have made the required number of chains for the pattern you are going to work. Count each V-shaped loop on the front of the chain as one chain stitch, except for the loop on the hook which is not counted. You may find it easier to turn the chain over and count the stitches on the back of the chain. When working the first row of stitches (usually called the foundation row) into the chain, insert the hook under two threads in most instances.

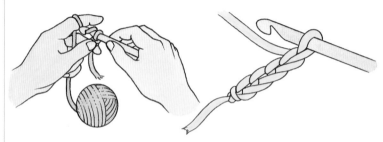

1 Holding the hook with the slip knot and the yarn in your left hand, wrap the yarn over the hook. Draw the yarn through to make a new loop and complete the first chain stitch.

2 Repeat this step, drawing a new loop of yarn through the loop already on the hook until the chain is the required length. Move the thumb and middle finger that are grasping the chain upwards after every few stitches to keep the tension even. When working into the chain, insert the hook under two threads for a firm edge, unless otherwise indicated in your pattern.

MAKING A SLIP KNOT

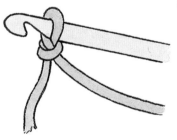

1 Loop the yarn as shown, insert the hook into the loop, catch the yarn with the hook and pull it through to make a loop over the hook.

2 Gently pull the yarn to tighten the loop around the hook and complete the slip knot.

ALTERNATIVE SLIP KNOT

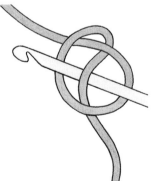

To work a number of stitches into a slip knot, you may need to make the slip knot so that it slides up from the ball end of the yarn rather than the tail. To do this, place the yarn ball at the left and the tail at the right as shown in the diagram, left.

TURNING CHAINS

When working crochet in rows or rounds, you will need to work a specific number of extra chains at the beginning of each row or round. The extra chains are needed to bring the hook up to the correct height for the particular stitch you will be working next. When the work is turned at the end of a straight row, the extra chains are called a turning chain, and when they are worked at the beginning of a round, they are called a starting chain.

The turning or starting chain is usually counted as the first stitch of the row, except when working double crochet where the single turning chain is ignored. For example, *ch 3 (counts as 1 tr)* at the beginning of a row or round means that the turning or starting chain contains three chain stitches and these are counted as the equivalent of one treble crochet stitch. A chain may be longer than the number required for the stitch and in that case, counts as one stitch plus a number of chains. For example, *ch 5 (counts as 1 tr, ch 2)* means that the chain is the equivalent of one treble crochet stitch plus two chain stitches.

At the end of the row or round, the final stitch is usually worked into the turning or starting chain worked on the previous row or round. The final stitch may be worked into the top chain of the turning or starting chain or into another specified stitch of the chain. For example, *1 tr into 3rd of ch 5* means that the final stitch is a treble crochet stitch and is worked into the 3rd stitch of the turning or starting chain.

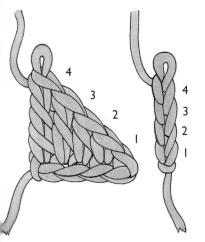

The box below shows the correct number of chain stitches needed to make a turn for each stitch.

DOUBLE CROCHET STITCH (DC) – 1 chain to turn

HALF TREBLE CROCHET STITCH (HTR) – 2 chains to turn

TREBLE CROCHET STITCH (TR) – 3 chains to turn

DOUBLE TREBLE CROCHET STITCH (DTR) – 4 chains to turn

STITCHES

WORKING A SLIP STITCH

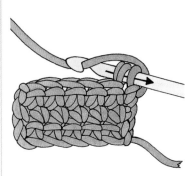

Slip stitch is the shortest of all the crochet stitches and its main uses are for joining rounds, making seams and carrying the hook and yarn from one place to another. Insert the hook from front to back into the required stitch. Wrap the yarn over the hook (yarn over) and draw it through both the work and the loop on the hook. One loop remains on the hook and one slip stitch has been worked.

WORKING A DOUBLE CROCHET

1 Begin with a foundation chain and insert the hook from front to back into the second chain from the hook. Wrap the yarn over the hook (yarn over) and draw it through the first loop, leaving two loops on the hook.

2 To complete the stitch, yarn over and draw it through both loops on the hook, leaving one loop on the hook. Continue in this way, working one double crochet into each chain.

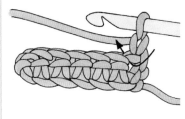

3 At the end of the row, turn, work one chain for the turning chain (remember that this chain does not count as a stitch). Insert the hook into the first double crochet at the beginning of the row. Work a double crochet into each stitch of the previous row, being careful to work the final stitch into the last stitch of the row, but not into the turning chain.

WORKING A HALF TREBLE CROCHET

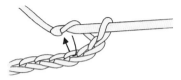 

1 Begin with a foundation chain, wrap the yarn over the hook (yarn over) and insert the hook into the third chain from the hook.

2 Draw the yarn through the chain, leaving three loops on the hook. Yarn over and draw through all three loops on the hook, leaving one loop on the hook. One half treble stitch complete.

3 Continue along the row, working one half treble crochet into each chain. At the end of the row, work two chains to turn. Miss the first stitch and work a half treble crochet into each stitch made on the previous row. At the end of the row, work the last stitch into the top of the turning chain.

WORKING A TREBLE CROCHET

1 Begin with a foundation chain, wrap the yarn over the hook and insert the hook into the fourth chain from the hook.

2 Draw the yarn through the chain, leaving three loops on the hook. Yarn over again and draw the yarn through the first two loops on the hook, leaving two loops on the hook.

3 Yarn over and draw the yarn through the two loops on the hook leaving one loop on the hook. One treble crochet complete. Continue along the row, working one treble crochet stitch into each chain. At the end of the row, work three chains to turn. Miss the first stitch and work a treble crochet into each stitch made on the previous row. At the end of the row, work the last stitch into the top of the turning chain.

WORKING A DOUBLE TREBLE CROCHET

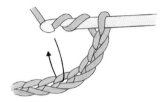 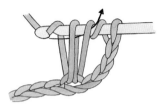

1 Begin with a foundation chain, wrap the yarn over the hook twice (yarn over twice) and insert the hook into the fifth chain from the hook.

2 Draw the yarn through the chain, leaving four loops on the hook. Yarn over again and draw the yarn through the first two loops on the hook, leaving three loops on the hook.

3 Yarn over again and draw through the first two loops on the hook leaving two loops on the hook.

4 Yarn over again and draw through the two remaining loops, leaving one loop on the hook. Double treble crochet complete.

5 Continue along the row, working one double treble crochet stitch into each chain. At the end of the row, work four chains to turn. Miss the first stitch and work a double treble crochet into each stitch made on the previous row. At the end of the row, work the last stitch into the top of the turning chain.

WORKING INTO THE FRONT AND BACK OF STITCHES

Unless pattern details instruct you otherwise, it's usual to work crochet stitches under both loops of the stitches made on the previous row.

WORKING INTO FRONT

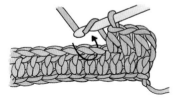

When instructions tell you to work into the front of the stitches, insert the hook only under the front loops of stitches on the previous row.

WORKING INTO BACK

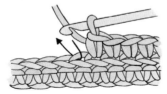

Likewise, to work into the back of the stitches, insert the hook only under the back loops of stitches on the previous row.

FASTENING OFF YARN

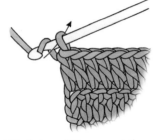
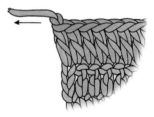

1 To fasten off the yarn at the end of a piece of crochet, cut the yarn 15 cm (6 inches) from the last stitch. Work one chain stitch with the yarn end and pull the yarn end through the chain stitch with the hook.

2 Gently pull the yarn end to tighten the chain stitch and weave the end in on the wrong side of the work (see below).

JOINING YARNS

Sometimes yarn is fastened off in one position and then rejoined elsewhere (to work an edging, for example). Also, if your first ball of yarn runs out, you will have to join in another. You can also join in a new yarn using the changing colours method.

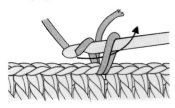

Insert the hook as the pattern requires, wrap the yarn over it, and pull a loop through. Leave a tail of about 10 cm (4 inches). Work one chain, and continue the pattern. If you are using a solid stitch work the next few stitches for about 5 cm (2 inches) enclosing the yarn tail, then pull gently on the tail and snip off the excess.

CHANGING COLOURS

1 To make a neat join between colours, leave the last stitch of the old colour incomplete so there are two loops on the hook and wrap the new colour around the hook.

2 Draw the new colour through to complete the stitch and continue working in the new colour. The illustrations show a colour change in a row of treble crochet stitches – the method is the same for double crochet and other stitches.

WEAVING A YARN END ALONG TOP EDGE

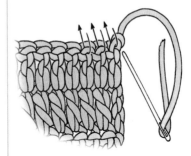

To weave a yarn end in at the top of the work, thread the end in a large yarn needle. Weave the end through several stitches on the wrong side of the work. Trim the remaining yarn.

WEAVING A YARN END ALONG LOWER EDGE

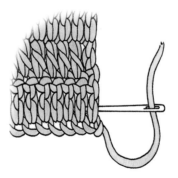

To weave a yarn end in along the lower edge, thread the end in a yarn needle and draw it through several stitches on the wrong side of the work. Trim the remaining yarn.

TEXTURED STITCHES

WORKING PUFF STITCHES

A puff stitch is a cluster of half treble stitches worked in the same place – the number of stitches in each puff can vary between three and five. When working a beginning puff stitch, count the turning chain as the first stitch.

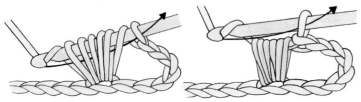

1 Wrap the yarn over the hook, insert the hook into the stitch, yarn over hook again and draw a loop through (three loops on the hook). Repeat this step twice more, inserting the hook into the same stitch (seven loops on the hook).

2 Wrap the yarn over the hook and draw it through all seven loops on the hook. Work an extra chain stitch at the top of the puff to complete the stitch.

WORKING BOBBLES

A bobble is a cluster of between three and five treble crochet stitches worked into the same stitch and closed at the top. Bobbles are worked on wrong side rows and they are usually surrounded by shorter stitches to throw them into high relief. When working contrasting bobbles, use a separate length of yarn to make each bobble, carrying the main yarn across the back of the bobble.

To make a three stitch bobble, wrap the yarn over the hook, work the first stitch, omitting the last stage to leave two loops on the hook. Work the second and third stitches in the same way. You now have four loops on the hook. Wrap the yarn over the hook and draw it through the four loops to secure them and complete the bobble.

WORKING POPCORNS

A popcorn stitch is a cluster of treble crochet stitches (the number may vary), which is folded and closed at the top. When working a beginning popcorn, count the turning chain as the first stitch.

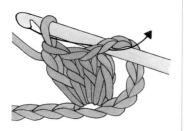

1 To make a popcorn with four stitches, work a group of four treble crochet stitches into the same place.

2 Take the hook out of the working loop and insert it under both loops of the first treble crochet in the group. Pick up the working loop with the hook and draw it through to fold the group of stitches and close it at the top.

WORKING BULLIONS

A bullion stitch is formed by wrapping the yarn several times (normally seven to ten) around the hook and pulling a loop through. Bullions should be worked on right side rows.

1 Wrap the yarn (not too tightly) as many times as directed around the hook. Insert the hook where required and pull through a loop. Wrap the yarn around the hook again.

2 Pull through all the loops on the hook. You can ease each loop in turn off the hook, rather than try to pull through all of them at once.

WORKING AROUND THE POST

This technique creates raised stitches by inserting the hook around the post (stem) of the stitch below, from the front or the back.

FRONT POST TREBLE CROCHET

Wrap the yarn over the hook from back to front (yo), insert the hook from the front to the back at right of the next stitch, then bring it to the front at the left of the same stitch. Complete the stitch in the usual way.

BACK POST TREBLE CROCHET

Wrap the yarn over the hook, insert the hook from the back to the front at right of the next stitch, then take it back again at the left of the same stitch. Complete the stitch in the usual way.

WORKING SPIKE STITCHES

Spikes are made by inserting the hook one or more rows below the previous row, either directly below the next stitch or to the right or left.

To work a double crochet spike stitch, insert the hook as directed by the pattern, wrap the yarn over the hook and draw through, lengthening the loop to the height of the working row, then complete the stitch.

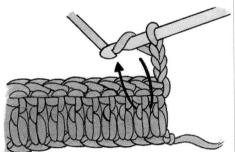

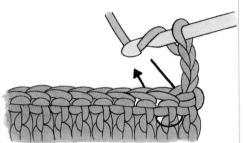

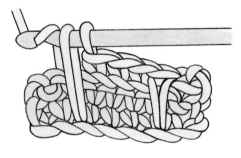

MAKING A FRINGE

You can make a fringe directly into a garment edge or first work one or more rows of double crochet edging around the garment to give a firm edge.

Cut the yarn twice the required length of the fringe plus a little extra length to account for the knot. Take a number of lengths (as stated in the pattern) and fold in half. Insert a large hook through the crochet edge from back to front and draw the folded end of the yarn through to make a loop. Hook the ends through the loop and gently tighten the knot. Repeat at regular intervals along the crochet edge and then trim the ends evenly with sharp scissors.

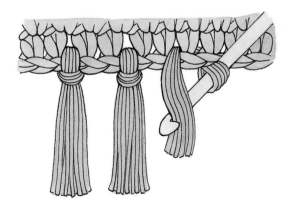

WORKING IN ROUNDS

Motifs worked in rounds are worked outwards from a central ring of chains called a foundation ring.

MAKING A FOUNDATION RING

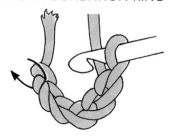

Work a short length of foundation chain (page 114) as specified in the pattern. Join the chains into a ring by working a slip stitch into the first stitch of the foundation chain.

WORKING INTO THE RING

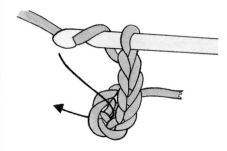

I Work the number of turning chains specified in the pattern – three chains are shown here (counting as a treble crochet stitch). Inserting the hook into the space at the centre of the ring each time, work the number of stitches specified in the pattern into the ring. Count the stitches at the end of the round to check you have worked the correct number.

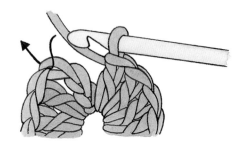

2 Join the first and last stitches of the round together by working a slip stitch into the top of the turning chain.

FINISHING OFF THE FINAL ROUND

To make a neat edge, finish off the final round by using this method of sewing the first and last stitches together in preference to the slip stitch joining method shown above.

I Cut the yarn, leaving an end of about 10 cm (4 inches) and draw it through the last stitch. With right side facing, thread the end in a large yarn needle and take it under both loops of the stitch next to the turning chain.

2 Pull the needle through and insert it into the centre of the last stitch of the round. On the wrong side, pull the needle through to complete the stitch, adjust the length of the stitch to close the round, then weave in the end on the wrong side in the usual way.

THREE-DIMENSIONAL MOTIFS

Initially, three-dimensional flower motifs seem a little tricky to work until you get the hang of holding the previously worked petals out of the way so you can work the foundation chains for the next layer directly behind them. This is one of those 'practise makes perfect' techniques so don't give up if your first few rows of petals don't look very neat. Try using a size smaller hook to work the chains, then change back to the normal size when making the petals. This makes it easier to insert the hook between the petals when joining the chains.

MAKING CROCHET BUTTONS

Crochet buttons are fun to make, whether ball buttons or flat ring buttons, and they can be made to match or contrast in colour with a garment or pillow cover.

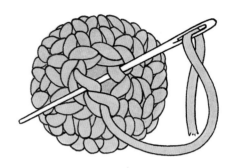

MAKING A BALL BUTTON

1 Work a ball button over a bead or a small ball of stuffing. Using a smaller hook than suggested for the yarn you are using, ch 2, then work 4 dc into the first ch. Without joining or turning the work, work 2 dc into each stitch made on the previous round. For the next and every following increase round, work * 1 dc in first st, 2 dc into next stitch;

repeat from * until the piece covers one half of the bead or ball of stuffing.

2 Slip the bead or ball into the cover. Start decreasing by working * 1 dc into next st, dc2tog; repeat from * until the bead or ball is completely covered.

3 Break off the yarn, leaving an end of about 30 cm (12 inches). Thread the yarn into a large yarn needle and work a few stitches to secure. Don't cut the yarn, instead use it to attach the button to the garment.

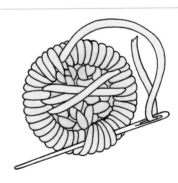

MAKING A RING BUTTON

1 Work a ring button over a plastic ring – choose a ring which is slightly smaller than the size you require for the finished button. Starting with a slip knot on the hook, work a round of double crochet stitches over the ring until it is completely covered.

2 Join with a slip stitch to the first stitch. Break off the yarn, leaving an end of about 30 cm (12 inches) and thread it into a large yarn needle. Sew a row of running stitches around the edge of the crochet. Turning the edge of the crochet to the centre of the ring, draw the thread up firmly and secure it.

3 On the back of the button, work strands of yarn diagonally across the button several times to make a shank. Sew the button on to the garment by sewing through the centre of the strands.

APPLYING BEADS

Before starting to crochet, thread all the beads onto your ball of yarn. If you're using several balls to make a garment, for example, the pattern instructions will tell you how many beads to thread onto each ball of yarn. When choosing beads, match the size of the holes in the beads to the thickness of your yarn; small beads are best on fine yarns, and larger beads on chunky yarns. When working with different bead colours arranged in a particular pattern, don't forget that you should thread the different bead colours onto the yarn in reverse order, so the pattern will work out correctly as you crochet. Beads are nearly always applied on wrong side rows.

BEADING WITH DOUBLE CROCHET

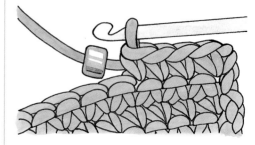

1 Work to the position of the first bead on a wrong side row. Slide the bead down the yarn until it rests snugly against the right side of your work.

2 Keeping the bead in position, insert hook in next stitch and draw yarn through so there are two loops on the hook.

3 Wrap the yarn over the hook again and draw it through to complete the stitch. Continue adding beads in the same way across the row, following the pattern instructions.

APPLYING SEQUINS

Sequins can be applied to a background of double crochet in a similar way to beads. Round sequins are the best ones to use, either flat or cup-shaped types. As a general rule, thread sequins onto your yarn in the same way as beads.

When crocheting with cup-shaped sequins, make sure you thread them onto the yarn so the convex side of each sequin faces the same way towards the ball of yarn. When crocheted, the 'cup' should face away from the crochet fabric, in order to show the sequin from the best advantage and to prevent the sequin damaging the crochet.

ADDING SEQUINS TO DOUBLE CROCHET

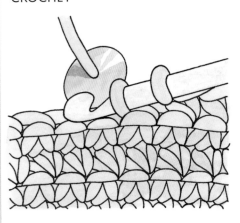

I Work to the position of the first sequin on a wrong side row. Work the first stage of the double crochet, leaving two loops on the hook. Slide the sequin down the yarn until it rests snugly against the right side of your work. Remember, if you're using cup-shaped sequins, the convex side (the bottom of the 'cup') should be next to the fabric.

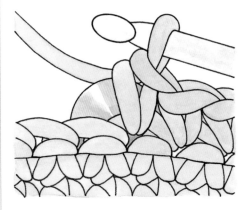

2 Keeping the sequin in position, wrap the yarn round the hook and draw it through to complete the stitch. Continue adding sequins in the same way across the row, following the pattern instructions.

WEB RESOURCES

The Craft Yarn Council:
www.craftyarncouncil.com

The Crochet Guild of America:
www.crochet.org

Craft Australia: www.craftaus.com.au

SELECTED SUPPLIERS
www.buy-mail.co.uk
www.coatscrafts.co.uk
www.colourway.co.uk
www.coolwoolz.co.uk
www.designeryarns.uk.com
www.diamondyarns.com
www.ethknits.co.uk
www.e-yarn.com
www.handworksgallery.com
www.hantex.co.uk
www.kangaroo.uk.com
www.karpstyles.ca
www.knitrowan.com
(features worldwide list of stockists of Rowan yarns)
www.knittersdream.com
www.knittingfever.com
www.knitwellwools.co.uk
www.lacis.com
www.maggiescrochet.com
www.mcadirect.com
www.patternworks.com
www.patonsyarns.com
www.personalthreads.com
www.letsknit.com
www.shetland-wool-brokers-zetnet.co.uk
www.sirdar.co.uk
www.spinningayarn.com
www.theknittinggarden.com
www.upcountry.co.uk
www.yarncompany.com
www.yarnexpressions.com
www.yarnmarket.com

MEASURING TENSION

Most crochet patterns recommend a 'tension'. This is the number of stitches (or pattern repeats) and rows to a given measurement (usually 10 cm or 4 inches). For your work to be the correct size, you must match this tension as closely as possible. To work out a design of your own, you need to measure your tension to calculate the stitches and rows required.

The hook size recommended by any pattern or ball band is only a suggestion. Tension depends not only on the hook and yarn but also on personal technique.

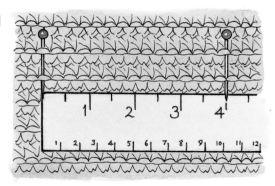

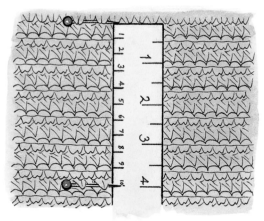

1 Work a piece of crochet about 15 cm (6 inches) square, using the hook, yarn and stitch pattern required. Only iron if this is recommended on the ball band. Lay the sample flat and place two pins 10 cm (4 inches) apart along the same row, near the centre. Count the stitches (or pattern repeats) between them.

2 Then place two pins 10 cm (4 inches) apart on a vertical pattern line near the centre and count the number of rows between them.
If you have too many stitches (or pattern repeats) or rows to 10 cm (4 inches), your work is too tight; repeat the process with another sample made with a larger hook. If you have too few stitches (or pattern repeats) or rows, your work is too loose; try a smaller hook. It is usually more important to match the number of stitches exactly, rather than the number of rows.

BLOCKING

Crochet often needs to be blocked before assembly, to 'set' the stitches and give a professional finish.
   Always follow the guidance given on the ball band, as some fibres can be spoiled by heat and moisture.

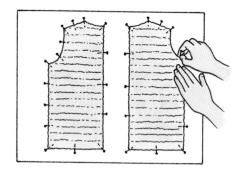

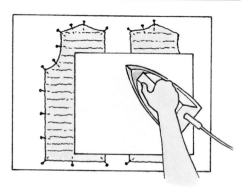

1 Lay each piece right side down on a well-padded surface. With rows straight, pin the pieces in place; inserting pins evenly all around at right angles to the edges. If necessary, ease the piece gently to size, checking the measurements. (Matching pieces, such as the two garment fronts shown here, may be pinned out side by side.)

2 Check the yarn band for ironing instructions. For natural fibres, such as wool or cotton, a clean damp cloth and a warm iron are usually suitable. Lift and replace the iron lightly, do not rub. Leave to cool and dry completely before removing the pins. After assembly, iron the seams gently.

Some yarns (such as some synthetics) should not be ironed: pin out the work as above, mist with cold water and leave to dry.

ENGLISH/AMERICAN TERMINOLOGY

The patterns in this book use English terminology. Patterns published using American terminology can be very confusing because some American terms differ from the English system, as shown below:

ENGLISH	AMERICAN
double crochet (dc)	single crochet (sc)
extended double crochet (exdc)	extended single crochet (exsc)
half treble crochet (htr)	half double crochet (hdc)
treble crochet (tr)	double crochet (dc)
double treble crochet (dtr)	treble crochet (tr)
triple treble crochet (trtr or ttr)	double treble crochet (dtr)

CROCHET AFTERCARE

It is a good idea to keep a ball band from each project you complete as a reference for washing instructions. Crochet items are best washed gently by hand and dried flat, to keep their shape. Crochet garments should not be hung on coat hangers, but folded and stored flat, away from dust, damp, heat and sunlight. Clean, acid-free tissue paper is better than a plastic bag.

STANDARD CROCHET ABBREVIATIONS

ch(s)	chain(s)	yo	wrap yarn over hook
sl st	slip stitch	rem	remaining
dc	double crochet	cont	continue
exdc	extended double crochet	alt	alternate
htr	half treble crochet	beg	beginning
tr	treble crochet	foll	following
dtr	double treble crochet	patt	pattern
trtr	triple treble crochet	RS	right side
st(s)	stitch(es)	tog	together
sp(s)	space(s)	WS	wrong side
lp(s)	loop(s)		
rep	repeat		

Ins — Cms
1 2 3 4 5 6 7 8
1 2 3 4 5 6 7 8 9 10 11 12 13 14 15 16 17 18 19 20 21

INDEX

A

abbreviations 125
accessories 40–45, 87–97
  ball button 40, 88, 100
  basic collar 44, 94
  beaded belt tie 45, 97
  close buttonholes 41, 90
  columns insertion 43, 93
  covered button 40, 88
  curved buttonholes 41, 90
  decorative cuff 43, 92
  diamonds insertion 42, 92
  double rings belt 45, 97
  fan collar 44, 95
  floral buttonhole 40, 89
  intricate lace collar 44, 95
  lace collar 44, 94
  loop buttonholes 41, 90
  looped picot buttonholes 42, 91
  mini circles insertion 43, 93
  picot buttonholes 42, 91
  picot collar 44, 96
  ring button 1 40, 87
  ring button 2 40, 87
  ring button 3 40, 88
  rings belt 45, 96
  spiked columns insertion 43, 93
  standard buttonholes 41, 89
  textured ruffle 42, 91
aftercare 125

B

back post treble crochet 119
ball button, making a 121
  see accessories
basic skills 114–115
  alternative slip knot 114

chains to turn 115
holding the hook and yarn 114
making a slip knot 114
turning chains 115
working a foundation chain 114
beads, applying 122
  beading with double crochet 122
belt tie, beaded 45, 97
belts see accessories
beret, embellished 108–109
blocking 124
bobble 118
bobble bolero 100–101
braids 26–30, 67–73
  angled chevrons 30, 73, 106
  blocks braid 27, 68
  bobble steps 29, 72
  bobbles braid 28, 70
  deep filet braid 30, 73
  eyelet braid 29, 71
  fans and columns 26, 68
  fans braid 26, 68
  fine blocks 27, 69
  jazzy braid 28, 70, 106
  layer braid 29, 71
  lazy fans 27, 69
  light and dark 26, 67
  long waves 30, 72
  luxurious braid 30, 73
  moving blocks 27, 69
  pyramids braid 29, 72
  random bobbles 28, 70
  ridge braid 28, 70
  shallow filet braid 30, 73
  sheaths braid 29, 72
  shiny shells 26, 67
  soft centre 27, 68

spray braid 28, 71
striped braid 28, 71
waves braid 27, 69
bullion stitch 118
buttonholes see accessories
buttons see accessories

C

cardigan, posy-edged 102–103
chains, turning 115
collars see accessories
crochet buttons, making
  making a ball button 121
  making a ring button 121
cuff, decorative 43, 92
cushion, frilled 104–105

D

double crochet stitch 115
  adding sequins to double
    crochet 123
  beading with double crochet 122
double treble crochet stitch 116
double-trimmed skirt 106–107

E

edgings 10–17, 48–57
  arcade edge 11, 50
  arch and picot edge 13, 52
  arches edge 12, 51
  beaded waves 13, 52
  beads and doubles 14, 53
  block edge 11, 49
  chain arches 14, 54
  deep ripples 16, 56
  floral edge 15, 55
  frilled edging 17, 57
  frilly edge 17, 56

fuzzy edge 11, 50
glitzy edge 10, 49
interlaced edge 16, 56
iris edge 14, 53
iris stitch edge 15, 55
large picot edge 11, 49
lattice chevrons 12, 51
layered chains 15, 54
mesh arches 14, 53
parallel lines 17, 57
picot arches 12, 51
posy edge 15, 55, 102
regular waves 11, 50
rhythmic edge 13, 52
scallop edge 10, 48
scalloped arches 13, 52
shallow ripples 16, 56
shallow scallops 13, 53
sharp chevrons 12, 50
shell edge 10, 48
shells and beads 11, 49
simply beads 15, 54
soft edge 12, 51
surface blocks 17, 57
undulating edge 16, 55
waves edge 14, 54
embellished beret 108–109
equipment 112–113

F

foundation chain, working a 114
frilled cushion 104–105
fringe, making a 119
fringes 18–25, 58–66
  beaded chevrons fringe 24, 65
  beaded filet fringe 18, 58
  beaded loops 23, 65

beaded triangles 23, 64
block fringe 19, 59
chevron fringe 24, 65
corkscrew fringe 20, 61
curlicue fringe 20, 60, 104
double crochet fringe 19, 60
double mesh fringe 25, 66
eyelash fringe 22, 64
granny fringe 25, 66
lattice fringe 22, 63
only beads 21, 62
open block fringe 19, 59
partly beads 22, 63
pearl leaf fringe 25, 66
popcorn fringe 23, 64
random fringe 19, 59
ringlet fringe 21, 61
slip fringe 21, 62
super sequins 20, 61
triple loop fringe 18, 58
twisted bullions 21, 62
twisted fringe 20, 60
undulating fringe 22, 63
front post treble crochet 119

H
half treble crochet stitch 116
hooks 112
    comparative crochet hook sizes
        113
    holding the hook and yarn 114
    useful hook/yarn combinations
        112

I
insertions see accessories

J
joining yarns
    changing colours 117
    fastening off yarn 117
    weaving a yarn end along lower
        edge 117
    weaving a yarn end along top
        edge 117

M
markers 113
materials and equipment 112–113
motifs 31–39, 74–86
    chain flower 38, 84
    chrysanthemum 38, 83
    circled lace 36, 82
    clover 31, 75
    conical shell 39, 85
    eastern motif 35, 80
    elegant petals 35, 80
    elegant rose 34, 79
    English rose 32, 76
    fan circle 33, 77
    flower silhouette 34, 79
    framed flower 37, 82
    golden leaf 38, 84
    golden pansy 31, 74
    intricate petals 35, 80
    Irish leaf 32, 77, 108
    Irish shamrock 31, 75
    layered rose 34, 78
    lazy frog 38, 85
    linked petals 32, 76
    marigold 36, 81
    pearl rose 39, 86, 108
    pinwheel 37, 83
    princely petals 32, 77
    shell flower 35, 81
    silhouette clover 33, 78
    snowflake 39, 86, 105
    square framed circles 37, 83
    star flower 36, 82
    sun daisy 31, 74
    sunburst 31, 75
    sunshine 32, 76
    three-dimensional (technique)
        120
    trellis motif 36, 81
    tufted flower 39, 85
    western motif 33, 78

P
pins 113
popcorn stitch 118
posy-edged cardigan 102–103
projects
    bobble bolero 100–101
    double-trimmed skirt 106–107
    embellished beret 108–109
    frilled cushion 104–105
    posy-edged cardigan 102–103
puff stitch 118

R
ring button, making a
        see accessories
rounds, working in
    finishing off the final round 120
    making a foundation ring 120
    working into the ring 120
row counter 113
ruffle, textured 42, 91

S
scissors, sharp 113
sequins, applying 123
    adding sequins to double
        crochet 123
skills see basic skills
skirt, double-trimmed 106–107
slip knot
    alternative 114
    making a 114
slip stitch 115
spike stitch 119
stitches
    working a double crochet 115
    working a double treble crochet
        116
    working a half treble crochet
        116
    working a slip stitch 115
    working a treble crochet 116
    working into the front and back
        of stitches 117

see also textured stitches
storage of crochet items 125

T
tape measure 113
tension, measuring 124
terminology, English/American 125
textured stitches
    back post treble crochet 119
    front post treble crochet 119
    working around the post 119
    working bobbles 118
    working bullions 118
    working popcorns 118
    working puff stitches 118
    working spike stitches 119
three-dimensional motifs 120
treble crochet stitch 116
turning chains 115

W
washing crochet items 125
web resources 123

Y
yarn needles 113
yarns 112
    holding the hook and yarn 114
    joining see joining yarns
    useful hook/yarn combinations
        112
    yarn types and weights 113

CREDITS

All photographs and illustrations are the copyright of Quarto Publishing plc.

ACKNOWLEDGMENTS

With thanks to Emily Hayden.

Thanks to DMC Creative World for kindly supplying yarns used in this book:

DMC threads distributed in the UK by:
DMC Creative World
Pullman Road
Wigston
Leicester LE18 2DY

Phone 0116 281 1040 for details of nearest stockist or visit www.dmccreative.co.uk

Thanks also to Rowan for yarns used:

www.knitrowan.com
(features worldwide list of stockists of Rowan yarns)

AUSTRALIA
Australian Country Spinners
314 Albert Street
Brunswick
Victoria 3056
Tel: (61) 3 9380 3888
Fax: (61) 3 9387 2674
E-mail: sales@auspinners.com.au

CANADA
Diamond Yarn
9697 St Laurent
Montreal
Quebec H3L 2N1
Tel: (514) 388 6188

Diamond Yarn (Toronto)
155 Martin Ross
Unit 3, Toronto
Ontario M3J 2L9
Tel: (416) 736 6111
Fax: (416) 736 6112
E-mail: diamond@diamondyarn.com
Internet: www.diamondyarn.com

NEW ZEALAND
Please contact Rowan for details of stockists.

UK
Rowan
Green Lane Mill
Holmfirth
West Yorkshire
England HD9 2DX
Tel: +44 (0) 1484 681881
Fax: +44 (0) 1484 687920
E-mail: mail@knitrowan.com
Internet: www.knitrowan.com

USA
Westminster Fibers Inc.
4 Townsend West
Suite 8
Nashua
New Hampshire 03063
Tel: (1 603) 886 5041 / 5043
Fax (1 603) 886 1056
E-mail: rowan@westminsterfibers.com

For stockists in all other countries please contact Rowan for details.